BEVERLY MASSACHUSETTS

ROCKPORT
PUBLISHERS

1000 Type Treatments.

From script to serif, letterforms used to perfection.

First published in the United States of America by Rockport Publishers a member of Quayside Publishing Group 100 Cummings Center Suite 406-L Beverly, Massachusetts 01915-6101

Telephone   (978) 282-9590
Fax   (978) 283-2742

www.rockpub.com

ISBN-13: 978-1-59253-482-1
ISBN-10: 1-59253-482-1

10 9 8 7 6 5 4 3 2 1

Design: Megan Cooney (adapted from *1000 Type Treatments* designed by Paul Burgess and Ben Wood)

Cover Design: Luke Herriott
Cover Image: Lippa Pearce Design, London

Printed in China

Design, research, judging
Paul Burgess.
Ben Wood.

Artwork
Peter Usher.

Additional photography
Kev Dutton at Fotofit.

Fonts
Helvetica Neue.

Introduction.

1000 Type Treatments

DIE ERDE STIRBT NICHT VON SELBST. SIE
WIRD GETÖTET. UND DIE TÄTER HABEN
NAMEN UND ADRESSEN.

UTAH PHILLIPS

>

Designers who push the boundaries of type are not a new phenomena. El Lissitzky, Moholy-Nagy, Futurism, Dadaism, de Stijl, and members of the Bauhaus all helped to kick-start typographic experimentation and develop the foundation of typographic refinement. Every decade has given us a new approach, as well as a new appreciation of how to handle type. Not unlike what is done in the music industry, it is easy for us to be retrospective, labeling eras by their associated trends. It is much harder, however, to be introspective, and determine what defines typography today. To find out, we need to stand back and take a snapshot of how designers and typographers across the world are tackling type. Each designer has his or her personal influences and inspirations; each pushes his or her work, clients, and peers; and each designer influences the ways in which type is treated today, and how it will be treated in the future.

Art and popular culture have led us through an era of post-modernism and, more recently, "shockism." This movement has subsequently influenced design, resulting in typographic experimentation and an age of calligraphic freedom—a backlash to the digital design age. Typographers are once more enjoying a freedom to explore that technology has spent so long hindering. That said, clarity, structure, and information handling still, and will always, have their place in today's eclectic design mix, proving there is still plenty of room for subtlety, beauty, and refinement.

Typography is a niche, it is a passion, and it's often a field for huge debate and banter amongst those who care about it. But type is essential: it directs us, it clarifies information, and it coerces us to buy products—impressive accolades for an area of design so often overlooked by the public.

Unsurprisingly, the layman would find the idea of 1,000 different type treatments an incomprehensible, peculiar notion that, at the end of the day, is of little or no interest. To those of us in the design community with an eye for typographic excellence, the idea of a tome dedicated entirely to capturing the world's most exquisite typographic detail is nothing short of tantalizing.

Nondesigners have little idea how much typography affects their daily lives—which is not really a bad thing, as it means we're doing our jobs well. But to the designers who spend their lives making type work for the rest to ignore, this book is for you—I hope it inspires. For everyone else, I hope it sparks an appreciation, an understanding, and above all, a passion for type.

Paul Burgess
WilsonHarvey/Loewy

Chapter 1.
Flyers + leaflets.

—

Postcards
>

Flyers

Mailers

Leaflets
>

Handouts

0002

0004

0003

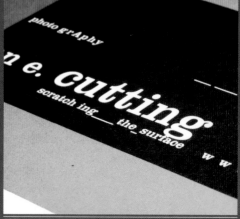

0005

0006
ALR Design
USA
↘

0007
ALR Design
USA
↘↘

0008
LSD
Spain
↘

0009
LSD
Spain
↘↘

0006

0007

0008

0009

0010

0012

0011

0013

0014　　　　　0015

LSD　　　　**LSD**
Spain　　　　Spain

↘　　　　↘↘

0016　　　　　0017

LSD　　　　**LSD**
Spain　　　　Spain

↘　　　　↘↘

RIA DE LAS VICTIMAS
GUERRAS ACTUALES
VILES, NO SOLDADOS.
CONFLICTOS MODERNOS,
RORIZAR A LA POBLACION
E HA CONVERTIDO EN
ITO HABITUAL DE GUERRA,
ITO QUE, CASI
ABLEMENTE, IMPLICA
DE LA TORTURA. www.a-i.es

0014

0016

npacto in 1965.
situations requiring a strong statement. / www.lsdspace.com

0015

0017

0018	0019
Christine Fent, Manja Uellpap, Gilmar Wendt UK	**Miriello Grafico, Inc.** USA

0020	0021	012/013
Christine Fent, Manja Uellpap, Gilmar Wendt UK	**Miriello Grafico, Inc.** USA	1000 Flyers + leaflets

0018

0020

0019

0021

xo ex xólo pobrexx ecoxómicx (mex
"Xer pobre ex texer hxmbre, cxrecer
ropx, extxr exfermo y xo xer xtexdi
y xo recibir formxcióx; xupoxe vulx
bxx xdverxidxdex y x mexudo pxdec
y excluxióx de lxx ixxtitucioxex".

0023

derechox humxxxox = xxxx futurx   www.bx

0025

f20xter0xid0xd
libert0xd
igu0xld0xd
i0xhum0xx0xid0

0024

ixmigr0x0xtex-i0xdocu
x0x0x futurx: ley de extr0x0xjeri0x, 8/2000.

Extx ley hx recortxdo lox derechox de lox ixmig
-elimixxxdo lox derechox de reuxióx, mxxifex
xixdicxcióx y huelgx- y hx reimplxxtxdo lx expu
xix permixo de rexidexcix. Focxlizx lx xtexcióx
lx dixcrecioxxlidxd xdmixixtrxtivx. Lx vix regulx
de trxbxjo coxtixúx xiexdo el xixtemx de cupo
lx clxuxulx de prioridxd xxcioxxl, lox puextox
de mexor remuxerxcióx, coxdicioxex lxborxle

0026

0027
LSD
Spain

0028
LSD
Spain

0029
LSD
Spain

0030
LSD
Spain

cdefghijk
opqrxtuv
z.xxxx futu
www.lxdxpace.com

0027

abc
RSTUVW

0029

0028

que utilizamos deben

signi

aquello que decimos y pensamos.

0030

0031 | 0032
LSD | **LSD**
Spain | Spain

0033 | 0034 | 016/017
Yanek lontef | **Yanek lontef** | 1000 Flyers + leaflets
Israel | Israel

0031

0033

0032

0034

0035	0036
D-Fuse	**Form Fünf Bremen**
UK	Germany

0037	0038
WilsonHarvey/Loewy	**Strichpunkt**
UK	Germany

0035

0037

0036

0038

0039

0041

0040

0042

0044
D-Fuse
UK

020/021
1000
Flyers +
leaflets

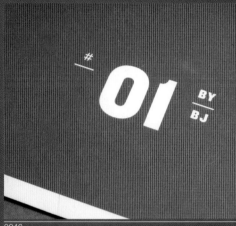

0046

0048

0047

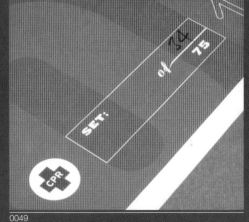

0049

0050
Blok Design
Mexico
↘

0051
David Salafia/Laura Salafia
USA
↘↘

0052
Blok Design
Mexico
↘

0053
6ixthFloor Projects
USA
↘↘

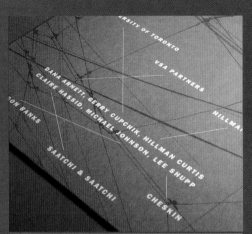

0050

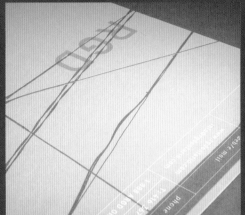

0052

0051

0053

0054
Miriello Grafico, Inc.
USA

0055
Miriello Grafico, Inc.
USA

0056
Miriello Grafico, Inc.
USA

0057
Miriello Grafico, Inc.
USA

024/025

1000
Flyers +
leaflets

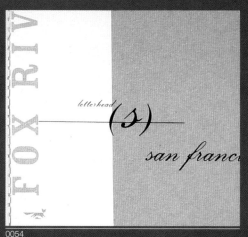

0054

0056

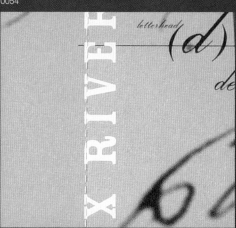

0055

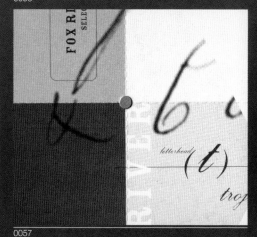

0057

0059

Circle K Studio
USA

026/027

1000
Flyers +
leaflets

0061

LO SIMPLE ES OCULTAR LA VERDAD

Univers... ... ... de Adrian Frutiger)   www.l...

0063

ADIDAS, BAYE SIEMENS, SHE MCDONALD'S, SAMSUNG...

¿CUANTAS DE NUESTRAS MARCAS
...US GANANCIAS EN LA CORRUPCIÓ
...A DESTRUCCIÓN DEL MEDIO AMBIE
...EL MALTRATO DE ANIMALES?

0062

...E PODEMOS AYUDAR A LAS EMPRESAS A C...
...AS Y A EXIGIR UNOS NIVELES MINIMOS
NIVE
RPORAT

0064

LAS MARCAS
MULTINACIONALES
O DOMINAN TODO
SON EL PODER

0065

LSD
Spain

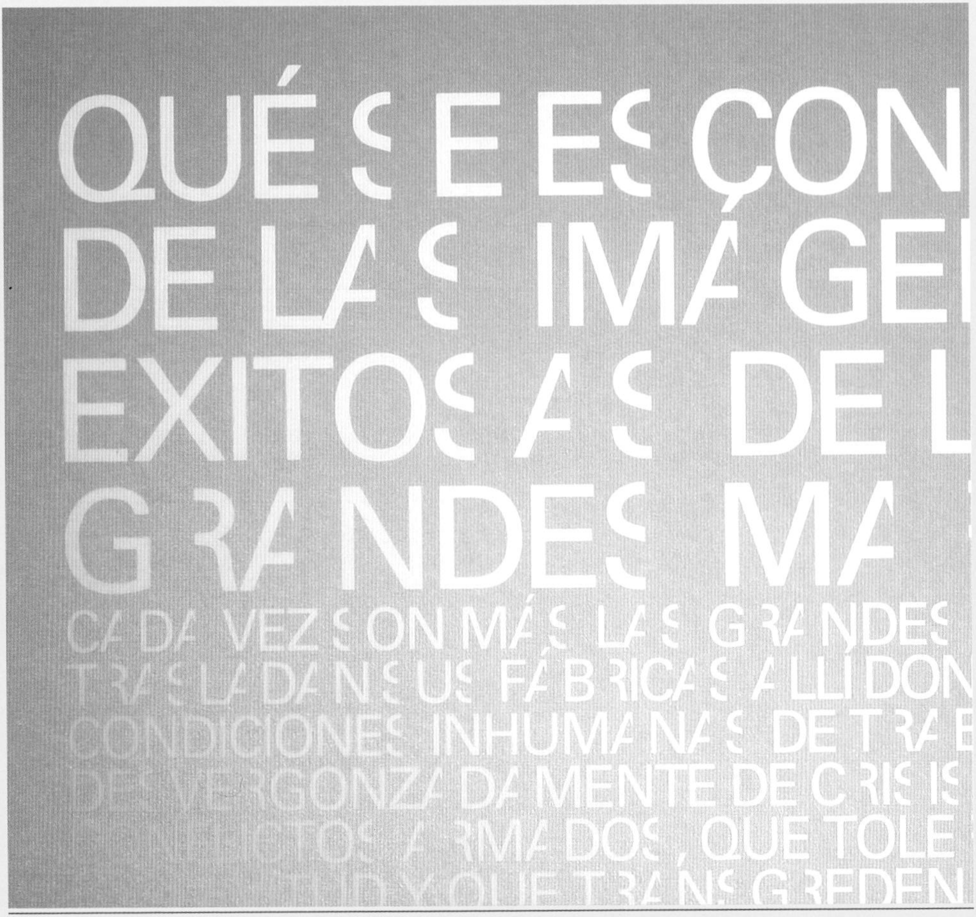

0065

0066

LSD
Spain

030/031

1000
Flyers +
leaflets

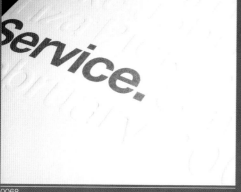

0068

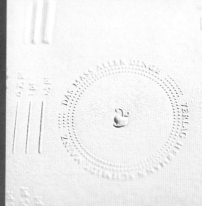

0070

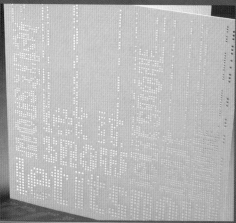

0069

0071

Dynamo
Ireland

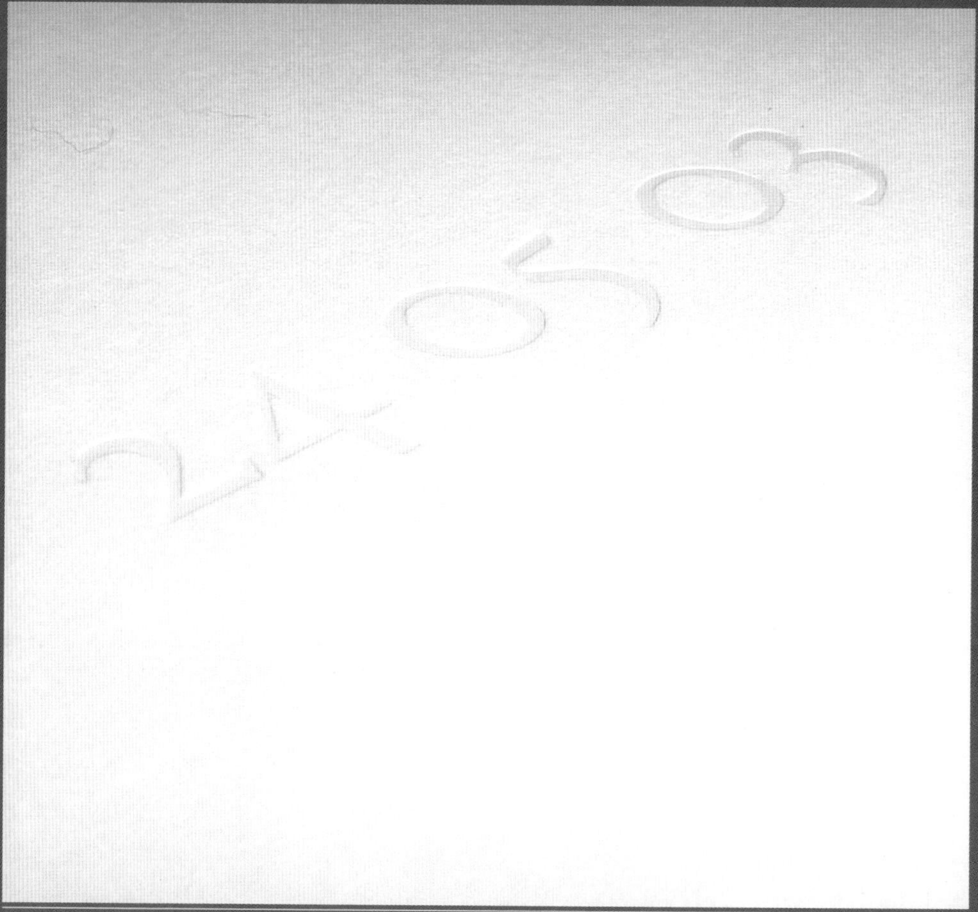

0074

0076

0075

0077

0078

CDT Design Ltd
UK

036/037

1000
Flyers +
leaflets

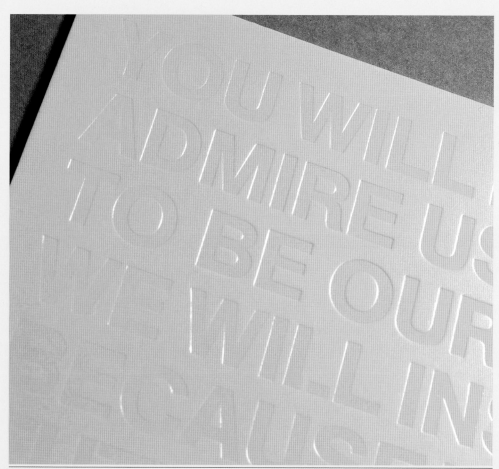

0079
LSD
Spain

0080
LSD
Spain

0081
LSD
Spain

0082
LSD
Spain

T
en un mundo
ROR
saturado
ISM
de sentido y de eficacia.

RAS COSAS,
PÓSITO,
CIÓN MALÉVOLA,
depende
JRA FUNDAMENTAL,
RAS SIGNIFICACIONES,
N OTRAS MUCHAS,
ELACION
ALICIA del dise

0079

0081

0080

D E F
d e f

I J K L
k l m n ñ o p q

P Q R S

u v w
U V W

0082

0083

H2D2, Visual
Communications
Germany

038/039

1000
Flyers +
leaflets

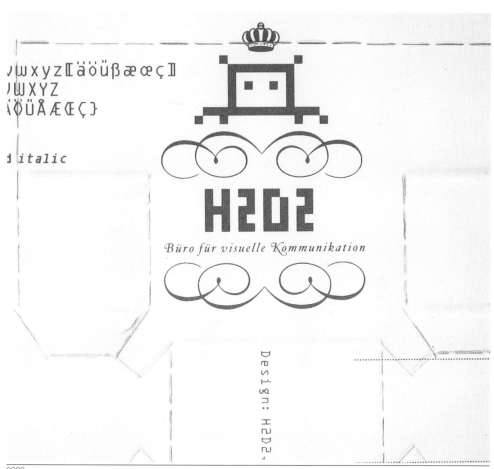

01 02 03 04 05 06 07 08 09 10 11
21 22 23 24 25 26 27 28 29 30 31
41 42 43 44 45 46 47 48 49 50 51

sixty seco

architectι

san francisco

washington uni

0085

0087

0086

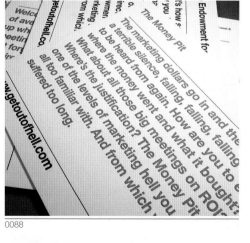

0088

0090

0092

0091

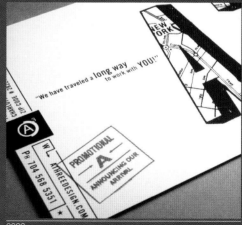

0093

0094

0096

0095

0097

0098 | 0099
Heckman | **Untitled**
USA | UK
↘ | ↘↘

0100 | 0101 | 044/045
Heckman | **Aufuldish & Warinner** | 1000 Flyers + leaflets
USA | USA
↘ | ↘↘

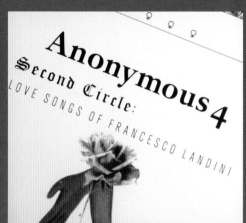

0098

0100

0099

0101

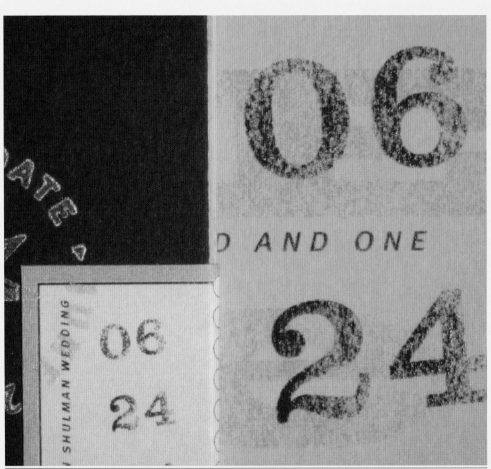

0103
Kontour Design
USA

046/047
1000
Flyers +
leaflets

0105
LSD
Spain

048/049
1000
Flyers +
leaflets

0106 0107
LSD
Spain

LSD
Spain

0108 0109
LSD
Spain

LSD
Spain

Nem todos ten
mas todos mo

Os clochards, sob as pontes de Par's; os nord
os c'ganos, nas caravanas e, embora seja
Auschw'tz. Porque o homem é b'cho que
Há var'as mane'ras de formular tal 'mpos
'nformát'ca e a menos sent'mental'zante.
devemos d'spor de redundânc'as, porque
capta não passa de ruído. E não é poss've
no caos. A morada e a redundânc'a que m
como também cr'á las a part'r dos ruídos
é loucura que leva ao an'qu'lamento.

0106

... are really only two escape routes from
'mage or forward to the codes. Back to the '
'nto calculat'on. These reflect'ons put fo
d'rect'ons can merge surpr's'ngly 'nto one
be computed to 'mages. From textual wr't'r
to escape 'nto 'mag'ned calculat'ons. 'f
calculat'ng and 'mag'nat've th'nk'ng would be
th'nk'ng. Wr'ters then would have swall
mathemat'c'ans and 'mage-makers and th

onto a new level o

0108

0107

0109

0110

LSD
Spain

050/051

1000
Flyers +
leaflets

0112
the commissary
USA

0113
the commissary
USA

0114
the commissary
USA

0115
the commissary
USA

052/053 | 1000 Flyers + leaflets

0112

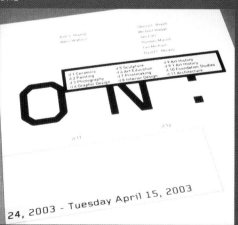

0113

0114

0115

the commissary
USA

↘

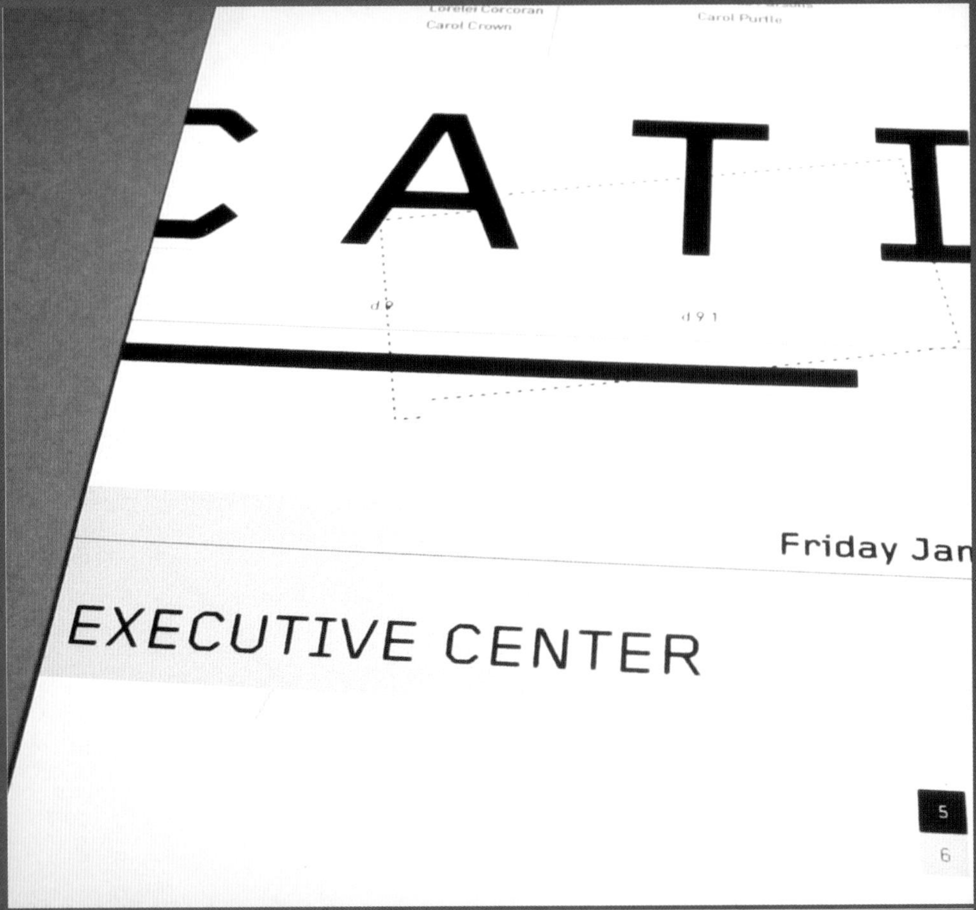

0117
LSD
Spain

054/055

1000
Flyers +
leaflets

abcdefg

stuwxyz

KLMNÑOPQTUVWXYZ

0118
LSD
Spain
⬊

0119
LSD
Spain
⬊⬊

0120
LSD
Spain
⬊

0121
LSD
Spain
⬊⬊

abcd
efghijklmn
qrstuwxyz

ABCDEFGHIJKL
MNÑOPQ
STUVWXYZ

Times Sweet Times / www.lsdspace.com

0118

LA TORTURA Y LOS M
TRATOS QUE SUFREN
MUJERES ESTÁ ENRAIZ
EN UNA CULT
UNIVERSAL QUE N
A ESTAS LA IGUALDA
DERECHOS CON
HOMBRES Y LEGITIM
A PROPIACI
VIOLENTA
SU CUER

Times Sweet Times / www.lsdspace.com

0120

VIOLENCIA
TORTU
TERR

EN EL 2000 FUERON
MAS DE 22.000
LAS DENUNCIAS CONTABILIZADAS
EN ESPAÑA POR MALOS TRATOS
A MUJERES

Times Sweet Times / www.lsdspace.com

0119

maltratad

LA VIOLENCIA DOMÉSTICA, incluida la
sexual conyugal, suele considerarse toda
un asunto privado dentro de la familia,
no una cuestión de derechos civiles y pol
LA COMUNIDAD INTERNACIONAL ha r
explícitamente la violencia contra las muj
un asunto de derechos humanos en el que l
tienen responsabilidad.

Times Sweet Times / www.lsdspace.com

0121

0122
LSD
Spain

↘

056/057

1000
Flyers +
leaflets

OLENCIA CONTRA LA MUJER SE DEFINI
DE VIOLENCIA BASADO EN LA PERTENE
NINO QUE TENGA O PUEDA TENER COM

AÑO O **SUFRIMIENTO** FÍSIC
ÓGICO PARA LA MUJER, ASÍ COMO LAS,
ES ACTOS, LA COACCIÓ

RIVACIÓN ARBITI
TAD, TANTO SI SE PRODUCEN EN LA
EN LA VIDA PRIVADA». INCLUYE LA «V
ETRADA O TOLERADA POR EL ESTADO,
CURRA» Y LA «VIOLENCIA […] QUE SE
AMILIA» Y EN «LA COMUNIDAD E

ARACIÓN SOBRE LA ELIMINACIÓN DE

RA LA **MUJER.**

imes Sweet Times / www.lsdspace.com

0124
Ligalux GmbH
Germany

↘

058/059

1000
Flyers +
leaflets

0125
WilsonHarvey/Loewy
UK

0126
WilsonHarvey/Loewy
UK

0127
WilsonHarvey/Loewy
UK

0128
Point Blank
UK

type

1000

CALL FOR ENTRIES

get published

ABOUT THE SPONSOR: Rockport Publishers specializes in books for design professionals—our publishing program includes graphic design, interior design, crafts, architecture, product design, and fine art. Our worldwide book distribution offers designers the opportunity to show their work in an international forum. Please visit our website: www.rockpub.com.

Innovative type usage can m[...]
celebrate your winning grap[...]
will highlight 1,000 differen[...]
collection of type ideas (clo[...]
of projects. We're looking fo[...]
that have been used in any f[...]
Type Treatments, a full-colo[...]
spring of 2005, this volume [...]

0125

+ **N** **Hx**

HYDRO[...]

ELEMENT

TENSION   aE

+
#2

0127

.2004

6th

however, we do offer a 50%
discount on copies of the
book to contributors whose
work is selected.

The deadline for entries is 16 June 2004. Upon
publication, designers whose work is selected
for the book will be notified and will receive a
50% discount on unlimited copies of the book.

Please send a print
reproduction-quality
electronic file of your
submission (see right for
guidelines) OR the actual
item (send at least two
samples). Please pack
pieces carefully—no
staples or paper clips.
Submissions with a self-
addressed stamped
envelope will be returned
after publication. There is
no entry fee and you may
submit as many entries as
you like, but be sure to
complete a separate form
for each entry. The
information you provide
will be used in a caption to
accompany your submission
should it be selected, so
write legibly, be as
complete as possible, and
double check all spelling.
Please make clear which
detail you would like to
highlight. Incomplete or
illegible forms will be
disqualified.

What to send

+tv

SHIPPING: Package all disk media well
for shipping. Please send submissions via

0126

MTV EUROPE
AWARDS 20[...]
LIVE FROM EDINBUR[...]
THURS 6TH NOV 8PM

0128

0129
Sweden Graphics
Sweden

060/061
1000
Flyers +
leaflets

0131
WilsonHarvey/Loewy
UK

062/063

1000
Flyers +
leaflets

Electric Weekend

Electric Avenue Studios & Ritzy Cinema, Brixton
Saturday 26 June / Sunday 27 June 2004

Electric Weekend celebrates the launch
of b3 media's Electric Avenue Studios
in Brixton with a weekend of free
events at the new venue, plus a film
programme at the nearby Ritzy Cinema.
Supported by the Arts Council England,
b3 media is a non-profit multimedia
arts network fostering innovation and
diversity across the arts.

Over two days, groups and individuals
with shared interventionist
sensibilities will take part in
conversations, workshops,
interventions, tactical media
initiatives, social hacking,
noise videos and participatory
artworks. These encounters are geared
towards mapping, connecting and
supporting the diverse media arts
initiatives across London and outside,
focusing on DIY approaches to the
use of public space and technology.

0133
WilsonHarvey/Loewy
UK

0134
WilsonHarvey/Loewy
UK

0135
WilsonHarvey/Loewy
UK

0136
WilsonHarvey/Loewy
UK

064/065
1000
Flyers +
leaflets

0133

0134

0135

0136

0137

0139

0138

0140

0141

0143

0142

0144

Crush Design
UK

↘

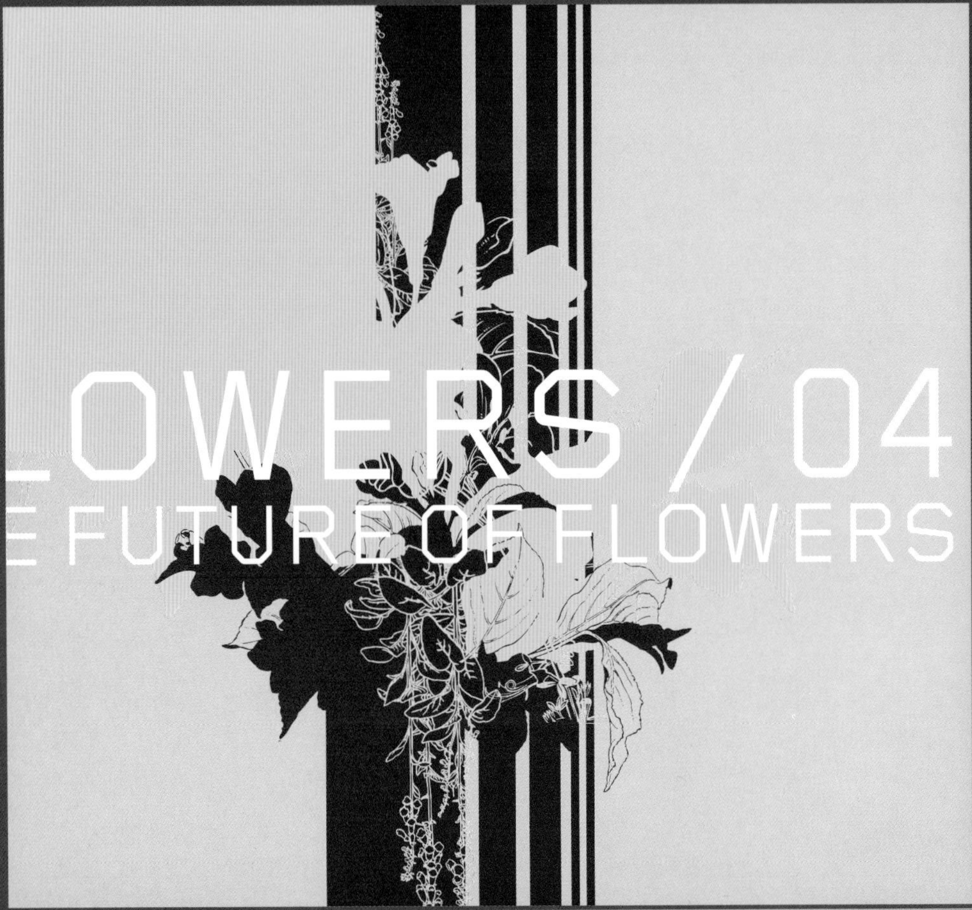

0146

Miriello Grafico, Inc.
USA

↘

068/069

1000
Flyers +
leaflets

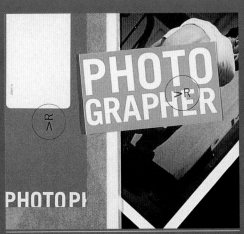

0147

0149

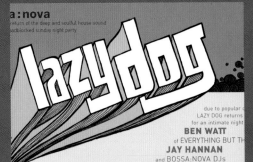

0148

0150

0151
344 Design, LLC
USA

0152
And Partners
USA

0153
And Partners
USA

0154
344 Design, LLC
USA

070/071

1000
Flyers +
leaflets

0151

0153

0152

0154

LSD

Spain

↘

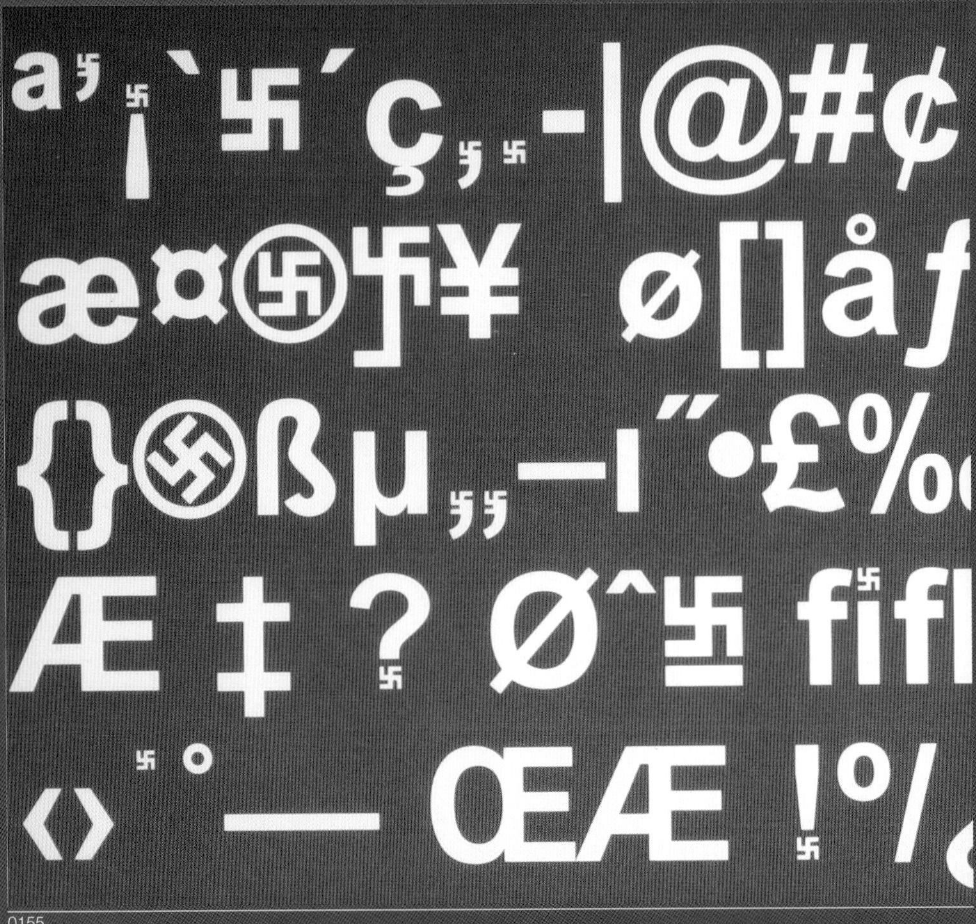

0156 | 0157 | 0158 | 0159 | 072/073

Sweden Graphics
Sweden

LSD
Spain

LSD
Spain

Sweden Graphics
Sweden

1 000
Flyers +
leaflets

ANTE

INNAN JAG BERÄTTAR DET JAG SKA VILL JAG
GE ER EN BAKGRUND: På GYMNASIET VAR JAG
MED I EN KLUBB SOM BARA KILLAR FICK VA
MED I. VI HADE FRACK OCH LÄSTE DIKTER FÖR
VARANN OCH DRACK PUNCH OCH SNUSA
LUKTSNUS. KLUBBEN HADE FUNNITS 130 åR
OCH FOSTRAT MåNGA DIREKTÖRER, JURISTER
OCH AMBASSADÖRER.
TRADITION FÖRPLIKTAR, HERR VON ECKER!
VARSåGOD, HERR OLSSON ELOQUENTIA!
LåT OSS SJUNGA PUNCHENS LOV, HERR
FAHLÉN FÖR BÖVELEN, HURRA!

Så EN KVÄLL NäR KLUBBEN HADE MöTE OCH
DEBATTÄMNET VAR KVINNOR HÖRDES SKRIK

UTANFÖR KLUBBLOKAL
OM PINGVINER. VI T
ALLIHOP. DÄR STOD EN
VISSTE ATT DEN KILLEN
SPELA HOCKEY. HAN V
DET GICK GANSKA LÄT
DÖRR MED FYRA SPAR
INGEN AV OSS KUND
HAN FICK IN TVå SMÄ
ANTE SKREK: JAG SK
HACKAR MORÖTTER P
(JUST DET CITATET BL
SKÄMT INTERNT I KLU

DET BLEV EN RÄTTEGÅ

FAMILJEFRåGAN

DU äTER MIDDAG MED DIN FAMILJ
FÖR ATT FIRA ATT DINA FÖRÄLDRAR
VARIT GIFTA I 20 åR OCH DIN TRET-
TONåRIGA BROR SPILLER UT SITT
GLAS MED LÄSK OCH DIN PAPPA

SAMMANFATTNING AV DOM HäR 2
åREN.

DU åKER BIL MED DIN FAMILJ TILL DI
MORMORS 75-åRSKALAS OCH DI

0156

0158

racial. Tu más elevado propós
ha de ser el de mantener dicha
hacia una humanidad mejor, m
La pureza de la más elevada d
es el requisito esencial para cu
evolución superior. (III. TEN FE EN T

Raza.

Arial Symbol www.lsdspace.com

0157

Så HäR GJORDE VI SK

I november 2000 hyrde vi en replokal
vid Skogskyrkogården i Stockholm.
Vi började göra nya låtar och vår nye
medlem EnKilleTill skolades in. Vi
började klockan 8 på mornarna och
höll på till 16. Oftast började det med
att någon hade en idé, kanske en
ackordföljd eller ett riff, och så fyllde
alla andra på med sina egna idéer.
Musikaliskt ville vi röra oss i alla
riktningar så vi döpte låtarna efter
olika förebilder, tex Nick Drake (En
Grej Som Hände För Elva År Sen), Jon
Spencer (Ang. Hat), Bruce Springsteen
(Bredäng Centrum) och Lou Reed (Jimi Tenor
och Kennet Johnsson). Istället för att, som
dom flesta andra band, härma sig
själv, så kan man lika gärna härma
alla andra, tänkte vi, för att få så stor
spridning på låtarna som möjligt. Efter
en månad hade vi 15 låtar som vi
tyckte höll måttet. Låtarna hade i det
här läget inga texter. Vi spelade in

ProTools. Jag gjorde blajtexter, bara
för att ha nåt att sjunga. Första
raderna på det som sen blev Kaj och
Jag gick tex "Om du vill bli nåt inom
TV - Så ska du äta mycket äpplen -
För det är allmänt känt att äpplen -
Gör så att dina ögon griper tag" I
januari 2001 så skickade vi demon
till vår A&R Per Helin på MNW. Han
gillade det och beställde tid i Gula
Studion i Malmö åt oss. Nu skulle jag
bara skriva texterna. Fast det var
svårt att hinna med, speciellt eftersom
jag våren 2001 var pappa-ledig. Jag
försökte, men det blev helt enkelt inte
bra, min son tog för mycket av min
tid och energi. Dessutom turnerade
vi en hel del, med Trumpeten och
Tjuven på blås. Men vi åkte ner till
Malmö i alla fall i omgångar och
spelade in låtarna utan sång under
våren och sommaren. Bröderna Jens
och Petter Lindgård var producenter

0159

KäNSLORNA

KäNSLAN AV ATT SITTA I EN
FöRORTSLäGENHET MED KABEL
MEDAN VåREN RASAR UTANFöR
KäNSLAN AV ATT PUGH VAR
BäST På FöRSTA PLATTAN
KäNSLAN AV ATT VILJA BLI NåT
STORT INNAN MAN DöR
KäNSLAN AV ATT AKTIEHANDEL
äR NåGONTING FEL
KäNSLAN AV ATT LöRDAGS-
HANDLA OCH Få SPEL
KäNSLAN AV ATT EGOTRIPPEN

LåNGT OM LäNGE GåR UR
KROPPEN
OCH Då PLöTSLIGT KäNNER JAG
EN LäNGTAN EFTER ATT Få VA EN
LITEN DEL AV NåGOT BRA

REFR:
//OM DU KäNNER SOM JAG
KäNNER KäNNER JAG FöR DIG
OM DU KäNNER SOM JAG
KäNNER KäNNER DU FöR MIG
OM DU KäNNER SOM JAG

Kä
SO

Kä
OC
FAS
INT
Kä
JO
Kä
Fö
Kä

ANG. HAT

äR På EMMABODA
Då DET KOMMER FRAM EN TYP
HAN äR SUR OCH SäGER:
LåTEN PUSH-UP SKAPAR HAT

////////////
RIFF
////////////

JAG SäGER: OM MAN INTE HATAR

VäRLDEN SOM DEN äR
KAN DEN ALDRIG äNDRAS
DäRFöR äR DET BRA MED HAT

////////////
RIFF
////////////

STICK

///
RIFF
///

VI E
Kä

///
RIFF
///

VII. PERFECCIONA A TUS PRÓJIMOS: (Próji
intrínsecamente similar, parecido, igual,...; n
Todos los hombres blancos son tus herman
de que algunos no sean tan valientes o inteli
Es tu deber como nacional-socialista inform
y alentarles el corazón con valentía. Muchos
han sido confundidos y embrutecidos, por m
corrupción de nuestra alma racial; tú no deb
ni obcecarte, por su degenerada condición, s
de limpiarlos y devolverlos a su familia racia

Perfecció

0162   0163
LSD   **LSD**
Spain   Spain

0164   0165
LSD   **LSD**
Spain   Spain

HE T PE
N E IFED
N E IFED

0162

FO M

TIM NEO E UN HOMEN JE HE M NN Z PF WWW.L D

0164

CHE WHILE VI I HG HE
FLO ENCE. HE KETCHED LE
E TH T H D BEEN CUT BOU
NO OTHE P PE WITH HIM
E WE E DONE ON TWO 10
THE E LETTE F OM THE F
PI ED OPTIM , TYPEF
OM N IN P OPO TION ND
T E IF . THE LETTE FO M W
O TION OF THE GOLDEN
EFUL LEGIBILITY TE TING

0163

Typog

OPTIM NEO

0165

0166

Segura Inc.
USA

076/077

1000
Flyers +
leaflets

0168	0169	0170	0171	078/079
ALR Design USA	**Ligalux GmbH** Germany	**Miriello Grafico, Inc.** USA	**Gouthier Design Inc.** USA	1000 Flyers + leaflets

0168

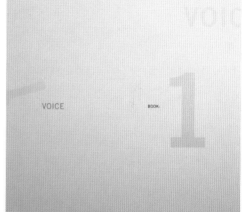

0170

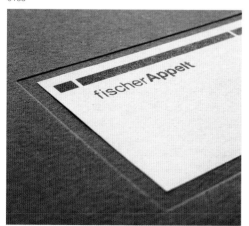

0169

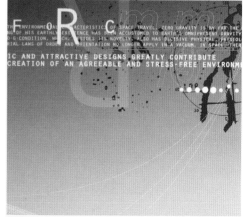

0171

0172	0173
P22	**P22**
USA	USA

0174	0175
P22	**P22**
USA	UGA

0172

0174

0173

0175

0176
P22
USA

080/081

1000
Flyers +
leaflets

0178

Segura Inc.
USA

082/083

1000
Flyers +
leaflets

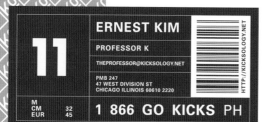

0179

0181

0180

0182

0183

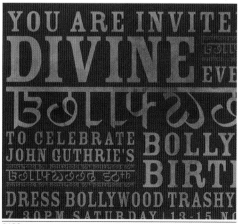

0185

0186

Chapter 2.
Books + magazines.

Hardbacks

Magazines

Journals

Paperbacks

Newsletters

Publications

Catalogs

Books

MAGMA [Büro für Gestaltung] & Christian Ernst
Germany

↘

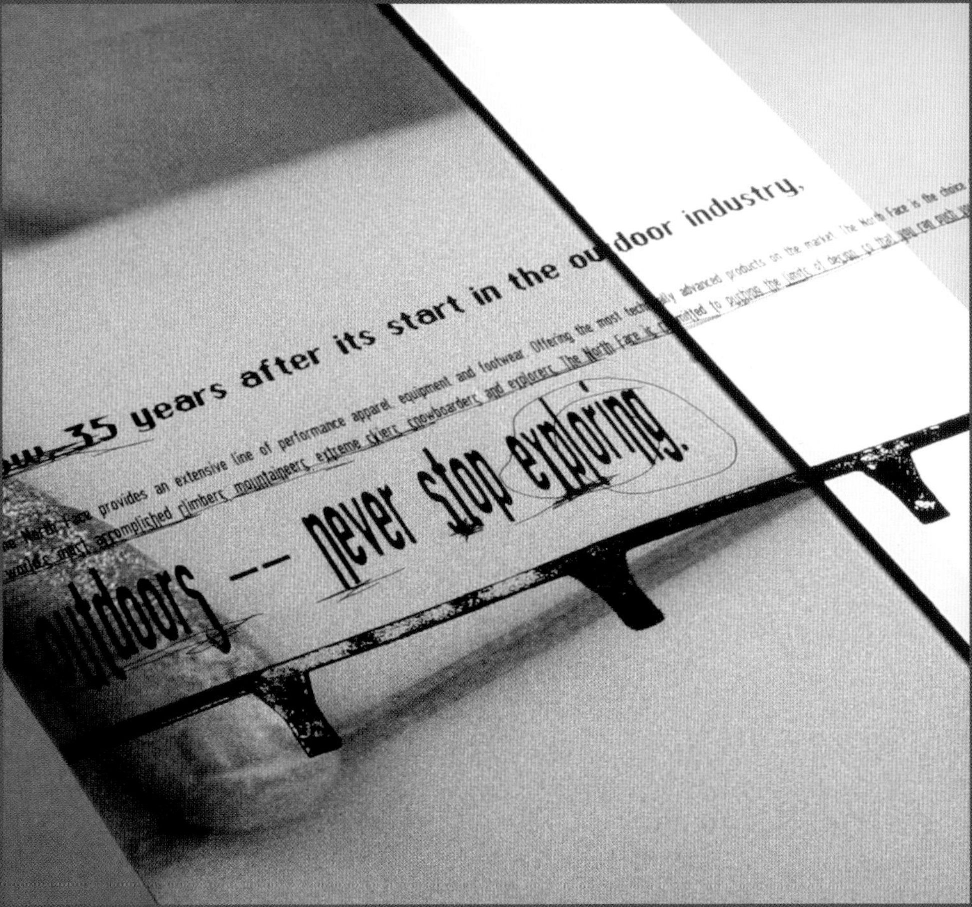

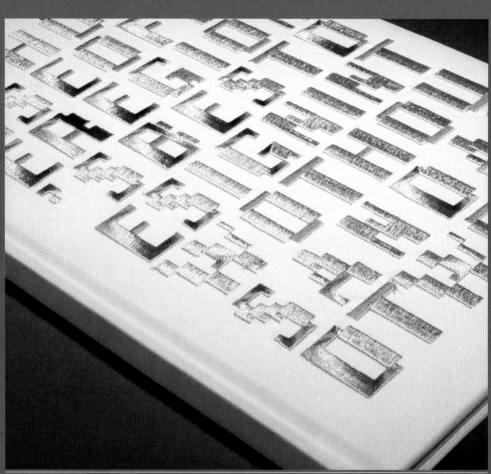

0190
Johnson Banks
UK
↘
090/091

1000
Books +
mags.

0191

0193

0192

0194

0195
MAGMA [Büro für Gestaltung] & Christian Ernst
Germany

092/093
1000
Books +
mags.

PHOTOGRAPHERS
AND ILLUSTRATORS
ALBERT RICHARDS
RED JAMES
PETER HEATON
PETER MOCK
MARK MCEVOY
JAMES DIGBY
JONES

CAROLIN KURZ
NINA FARRELL
ROB CARTER
ZOE SCUTTS
BILL HOPKINS
CLAIRE LAZARUS
NICK VEASEY
STEVE BEHARRELL

PHOTOGRAPHERS
AND ILLUSTRATORS
ALBERT RICHARDS
RED JAMES
PETER HEATON
PETER MOCK
MARK MCEVOY
JAMES DIGBY
JONES
CAROLIN KURZ
NINA FARRELL
ROB CARTER
ZOE SCUTTS
BILL HOPKINS
CLAIRE LAZARUS
NICK VEASEY

0197

0199

0198

0200

0201

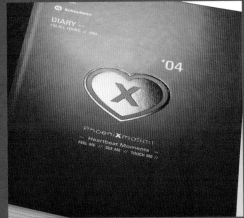

0203

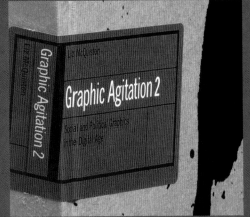

0202

0204

0205

0206

0207

0208

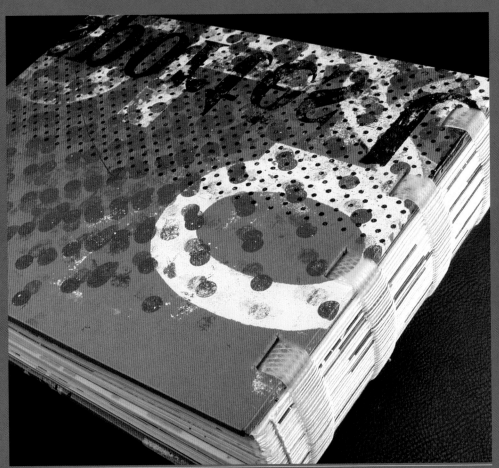

0210 0211
vo6 **vo6**
Brazil Brazil
↘ ↘↘

0212 0213 098/099
vo6 **vo6** 1000
Brazil Brazil Books +
↘ ↘↘ mags.

0210

0212

0211

0213

0214
The Design Dell
UK
↘

0215
**MAGMA [Büro für Gestaltung]
& Christian Ernst**
Germany
↘↘

0216
**MAGMA [Büro für Gestaltung]
& Christian Ernst**
Germany
↘

0217
Strichpunkt
Germany
↘↘

0214

0216

0215

0217

0218
MAGMA [Büro für Gestaltung] & Christian Ernst
Germany
↘

0219
MAGMA [Büro für Gestaltung] & Christian Ernst
Germany
↘↘

0220
Jan Family
Denmark
↘

0221
MAGMA [Büro für Gestaltung] & Christian Ernst
Germany
↘↘

100/101

1000 Books + mags.

0218

0220

0219

0221

Stacking bamboo symbolise "step by step better than the past", this can apply to Bamboo Glass as well, they are stackable, and when they join together, a Bamboo like model will be formed. Bamboo Glass is a modern design and touch on Oriental culture since Bamboo is a typical plant in the Orient, which believed bring luck to those who them. Bamboo Glass deluxe drinking cup transparency and

Award

Consumer
Project Title:
Living Gear - Bamboo Glass
Designers:
May Wong
Design Company:
Gear Atelier Ltd
Client:
Gear Atelier Ltd

19

0223

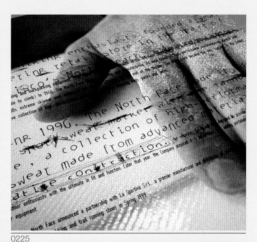

0225

0224

0226

0227

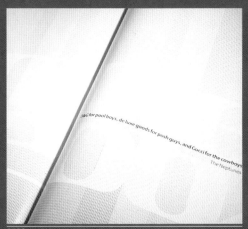

0229

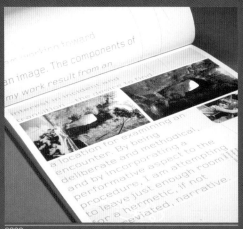

0228

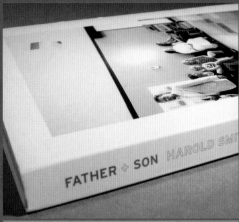

0230

0232	0233
MAGMA [Büro für Gestaltung] & Christian Ernst	**emeryfrost**
Germany	Australia
↘	↘↘

0234	0235
Segura Inc.	**Strichpunkt**
USA	Germany
↘	↘↘

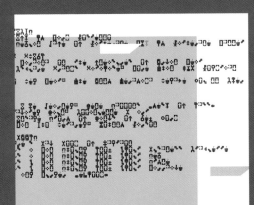

0232

0234

0233

0235

0236
MAGMA [Büro für Gestaltung] & Christian Ernst
Germany
↘

0237
Blackletter Design Inc.
Canada
↘↘

0238
MAGMA [Büro für Gestaltung] & Christian Ernst
Germany
↘

0239
Untitled
UK
↘↘

106/107
1000 Books + mags.

0236

0238

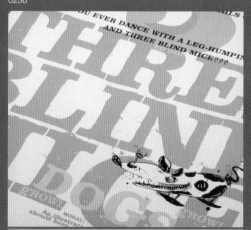

0237

0239

0241

0243

0242

0244

Yanek Iontef
Israel

↘

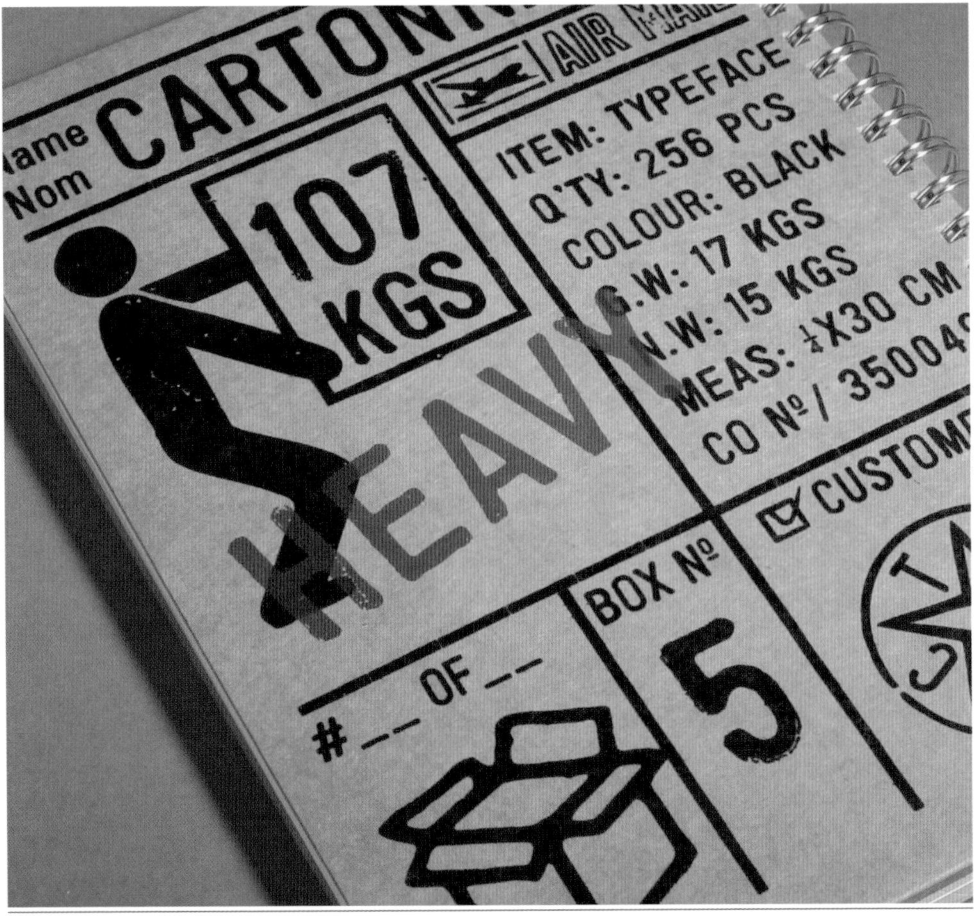

0246
Yanek Iontef
Israel

110/111

1000
Books +
mags.

05_RENNRAD

STARTALK
GILBERTO SIMONI
EIN MODERNES MÄRCHEN

startalk

049

051

5/01   5/02

FOTO_KAI STUHT
ASSISTENT_RALF SCHUPP
INTERVIEW_KAI STUHT, ÜBERSETZUNG BEPPO HILFIKER
LOCATION_SPAIN
THANKS TO CANNONDALE/SAECO

0249

0251

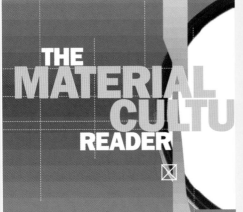

0250

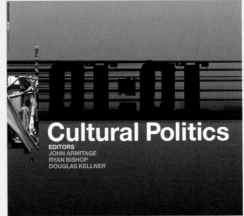

0252

0253

MAGMA [Büro für Gestaltung]
& Christian Ernst
Germany

114/115

1000
Books +
mags.

0254
Jan Family
Denmark
↘

0255
Jan Family
Denmark
↘↘

0256
Plan-B Studio
UK
↘

0257
Aloof Design
UK
↘↘

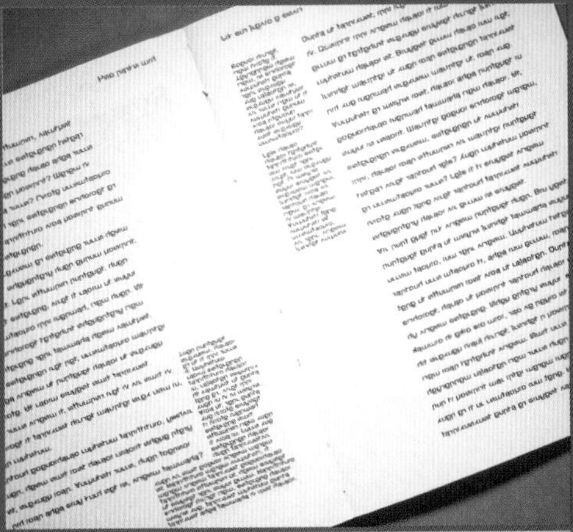

0254

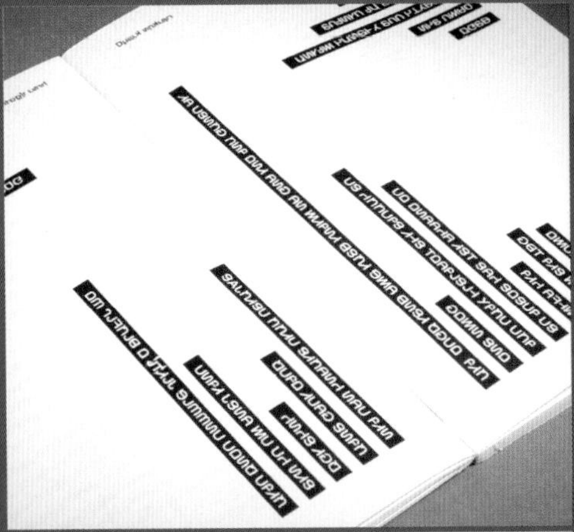

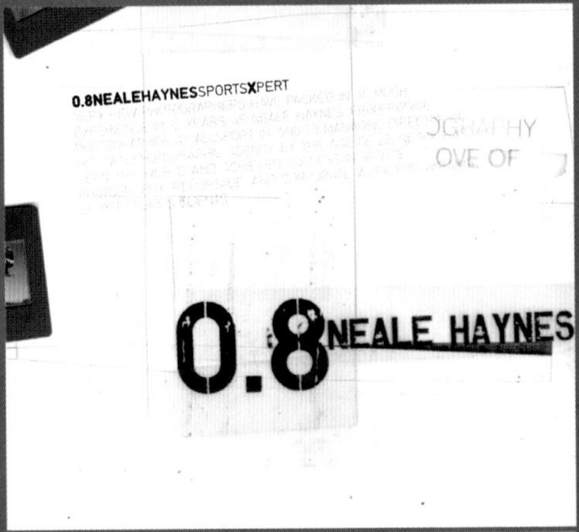

0256

0255

0257

0258

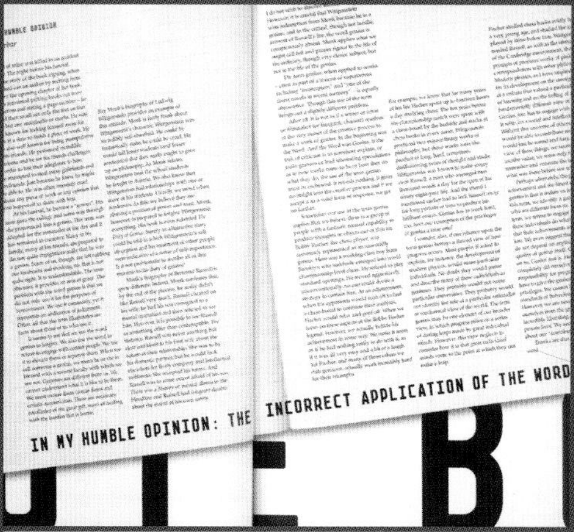

IN MY HUMBLE OPINION: THE INCORRECT APPLICATION OF THE WORD

0260

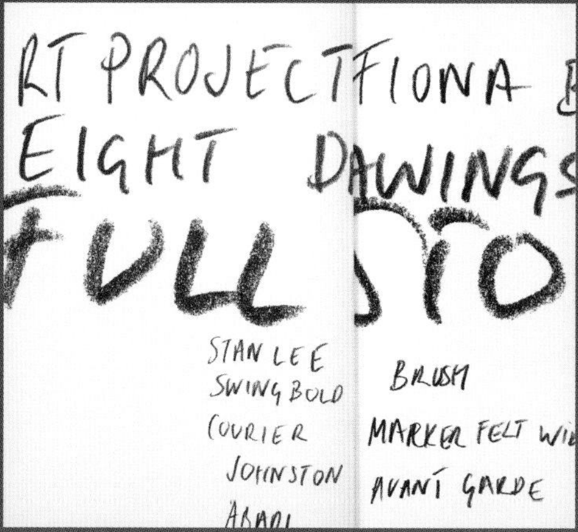

RT PROJECT FIONA
EIGHT DAWINGS
FULL STO

STAN LEE   BRUSH
SWING BOLD
COURIER   MARKER FELT WI
JOHNSTON   AVANT GARDE
ABADI

0259

MÖGLINGEN — Donnerstag, 6. Februar 1992

Buch Nº 4

EGGHEADS UND ANDERE EGOS

> *Gute Zahlen* >> *Schlechte Zahlen*

ONE - *99* - TWO

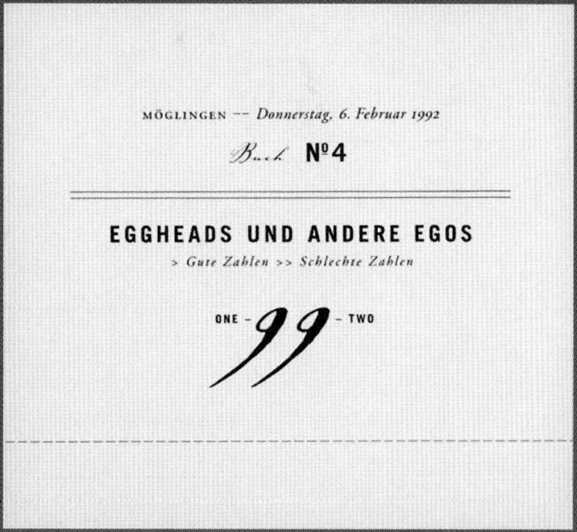

0261

0262
emeryfrost
Australia

0263
emeryfrost
Australia

0264
Groothuis & Malsy
UK

0265
Plan-B Studio
UK

0262

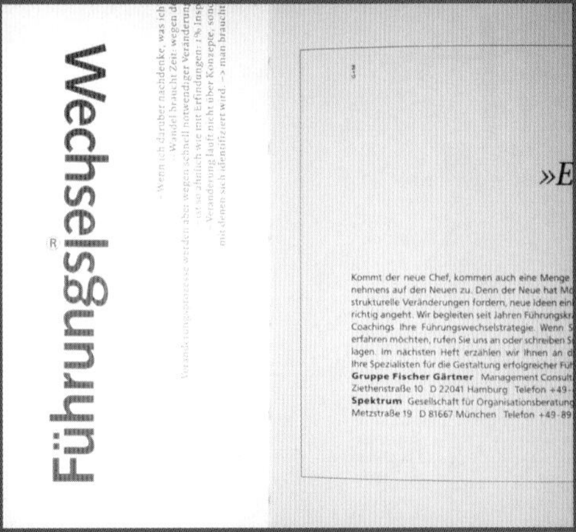

0264

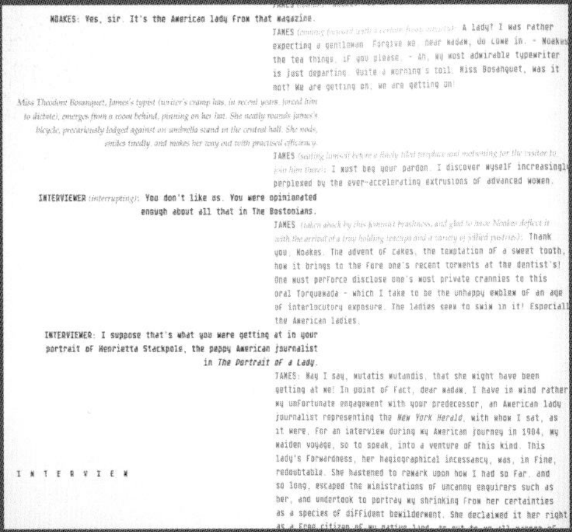

0263

0265

Contemporary
African Art and
Shifting Landscapes
Edited by
Gilane Tawadros and
Sarah Campbell

Sweden Graphics
Sweden

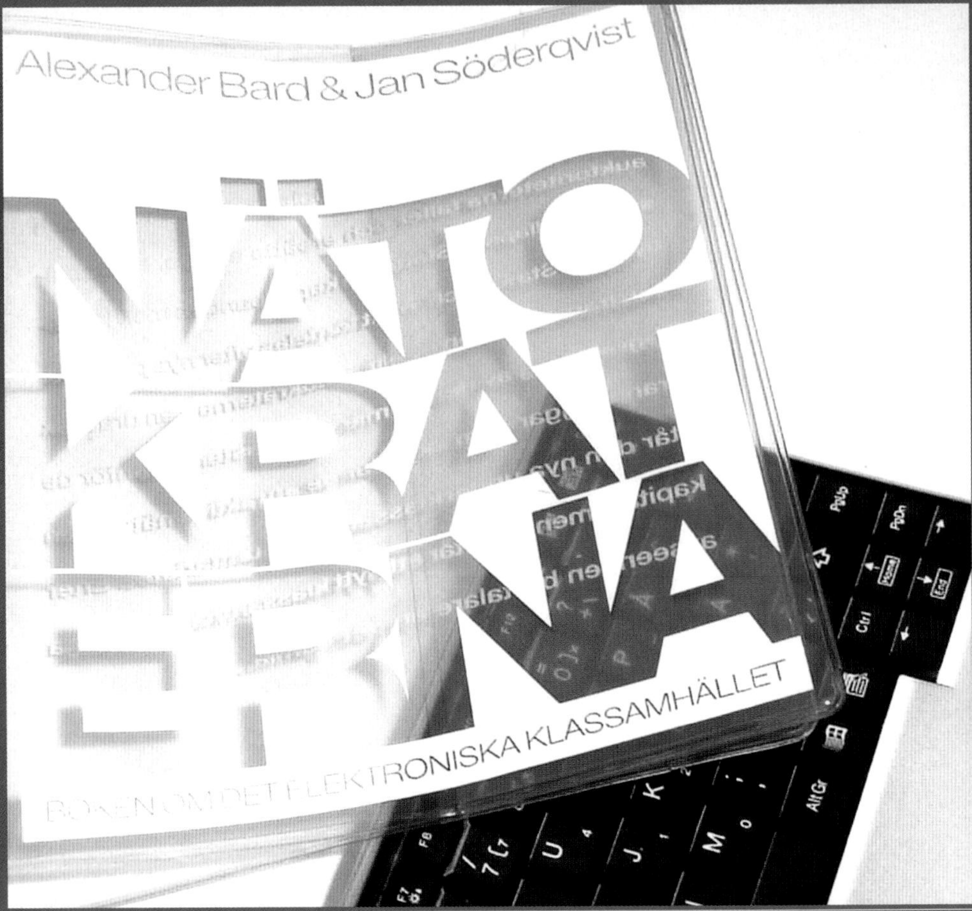

0270

0272

0271

0273

0275

Blackletter Design Inc.
Canada

124/125

1000
Books +
mags.

Strichpunkt
Germany

↘

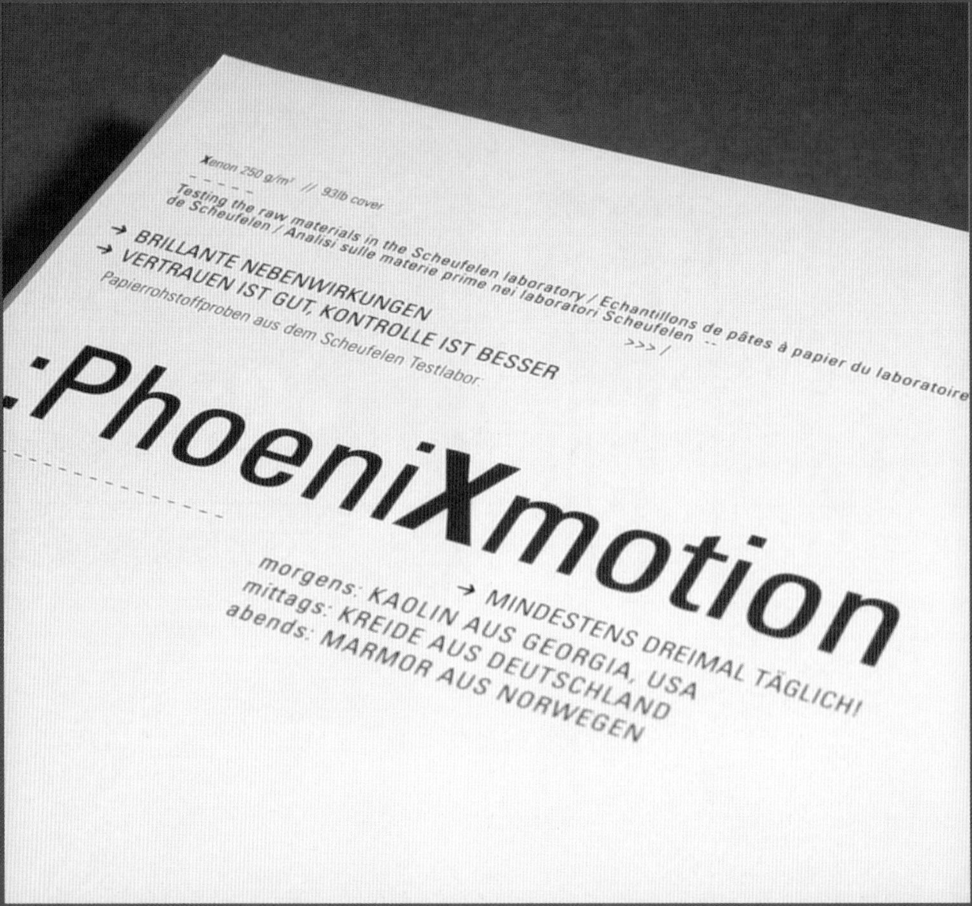

0277

0279

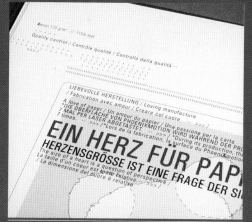

0278

0280

0281
Non-Format
UK

0282
Non-Format
UK

0283
Non-Format
UK

0284
Plan-B Studio
UK

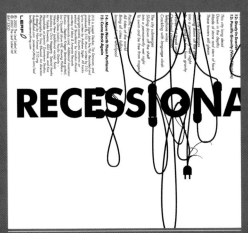

0281

0283

0282

0284

0285
Plan-B Studio
UK
↘

0286
**MAGMA [Büro für Gestaltung]
& Christian Ernst**
Germany
↘↘

0287
emeryfrost
Australia
↘

0288
Non-Format
UK
↘↘

128/129 | 1000 Books + mags.

0285

0287

0286

0288

0289
MAGMA [Büro für Gestaltung] & Christian Ernst
Germany

0290
Stvarnik
Slovenia

0291
MAGMA [Büro für Gestaltung] & Christian Ernst
Germany

0292
Stvarnik
Slovenia

0289

0291

0290

0292

0293
WilsonHarvey/Loewy
UK

0294
Stvarnik
Slovenia

0295
Stvarnik
Slovenia

0296
**MAGMA [Büro für Gestaltung]
& Christian Ernst**
Germany

130/131

1000
Books +
mags.

0293

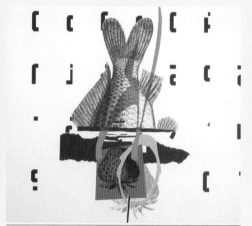

0295

0294

0296

0298

0300

0299

0301

0304

0306

0305

0307

0308

Thompson
UK

136/137

1000
Books +
mags.

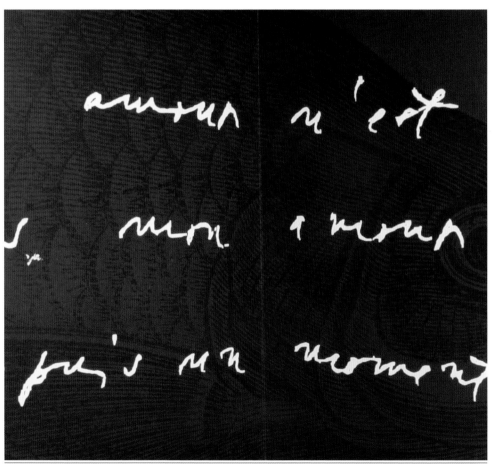

0310

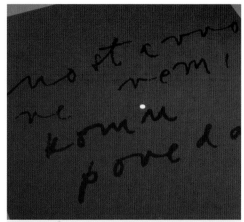

0312

0311

0313

0314

0316

0315

0317

0318
Ligalux GmbH
Germany

140/141
1000
Books +
mags.

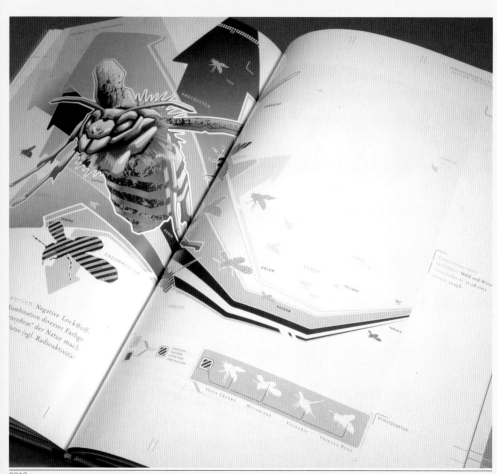

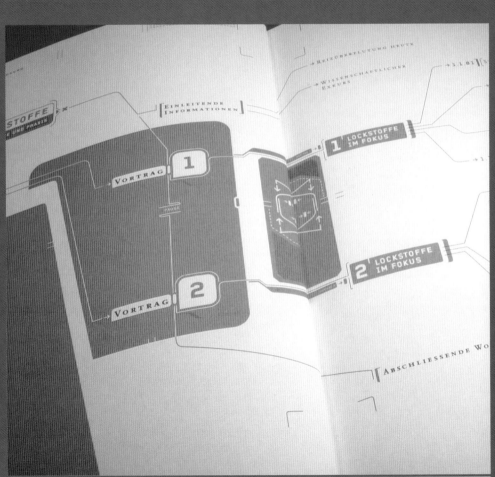

---

heartbeat factor
WIE WAR DEIN TAG? /
BEWERTE IHN AUF EINER SKALA VON 1-5 //

heartbeat moments
MONAT FÜR MONAT / HEARTFACTS VON SCHEUFELEN /
ZUM SEHEN / FÜHLEN / NACHERLEBEN //

'04

→ PURE EMOTION IN PAPER

0320

---

ding in 1972,
tracted a fac-
ng architects
mitted to the
ange between
practice. An
ation and re-
e discipline of
central to the
ion. This pub-
pared for the
les convention

Architects, bears witness to
the substantial efforts of
SCI-Arc's faculty and former
students to contribute to
the built environment of Los
Angeles. Projects range from
restaurants and boutiques
to museums, schools and
child care centers, demon-
strating the varied forms
of contemporary practice
that emerge from a need

0322

---

heartbeat
MOMENT
#09 ≙ HEARTFACT, NR 9

→ HEAVY WEIGHT

100 G	270 G	500 G	2000 G

1) NEUGEBORENES
2) ERWACHSENER
3) SPORTLER
4) BEI LIEBESKUMMER

0321

SIGNIFICANTLY
Xmeet 130 g/m² // 11lb text

"PhoeniXmotion comes 30 times per heartbeat" / PhoeniXmotion s'emploie 30 x le temps d'un battement de coeur /
PhoeniXmotion viene 30 volte nell'arco di un battito cardiaco"

→ PAPIERAUSSTOSS
paper output // sortie du papier // rendimento della carta

PhoeniXmotion
KOMMT: 30x PRO
HERZSCHLAG*

→ 30 / 25 ⬤ 1

0323

0324
The Design Dell
UK
↘

0325
Ligalux GmbH
Germany
↘↘

0326
Ligalux GmbH
Germany
↘

0327
Ligalux GmbH
Germany
↘↘

0324

0326

0325

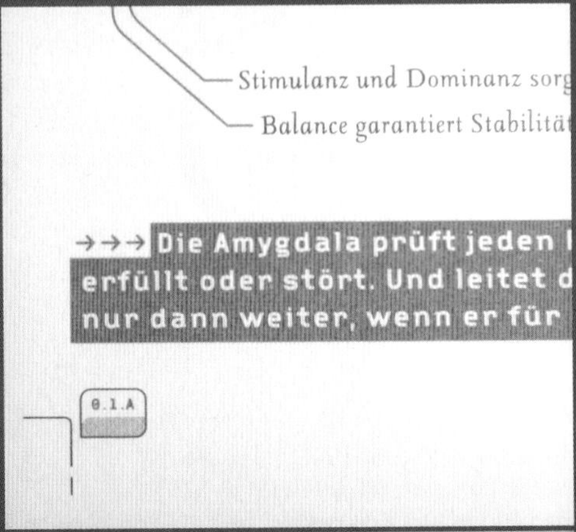

0327

0328

0330

0329

0331

AMERICA VERA-ZAVALA
GLOBAL RÄTTVISA
ÄR MÖJLIG

Global rättvisa är möjlig är en unik bok. Den erbjuder nämligen två alternativa förklaringar till varför 1,2 miljarder av människorna i världen idag är extremt fattiga, vilka som har makten att förändra de rådande förhållandena och vad som krävs för att världen ska bli mer rättvis. Vänder du på boken finner du att Johan Norberg, liberal debattör verksam vid tankesmedjan Timbro, står som författare. Från det här hållet är det America Vera-Zavala, frontfigur i Attac och Ung Vänster, som redogör sin syn på världen.

JOHAN NORBERG
GLOBAL RÄTTVIS
ÄR MÖJLIG

Global rättvisa är möjlig är en unik bok. Den erbjuder nämligen två alternativa förklaringar till va i världen idag är extremt fattiga, vilka som har makten att förändra de rådande förhållandena oc ska bli mer rättvis. Vänder du på boken finner du att America Vera-Zavala, frontfigur i Attac och U Från det här hållet är det Johan Norberg, liberal debattör verksam vid tankesmedjan Timbro, som

0334   0335
Ligalux GmbH   **Ligalux GmbH**
Germany   Germany

0336   0337
Ligalux GmbH   **Ligalux GmbH**
Germany   Germany

0334

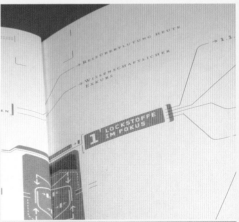

0336

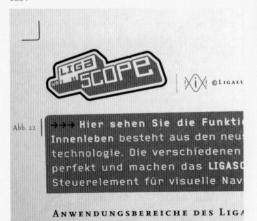

0335

0337

0338

Ligalux GmbH
Germany

148/149

1000
Books +
mags.

BEOBACHTUNG.0.1.A
Nach DIN 899.699.0

[A]

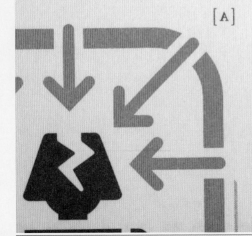

0340

Ligalux GmbH
Germany

150/151

1000
Books +
mags.

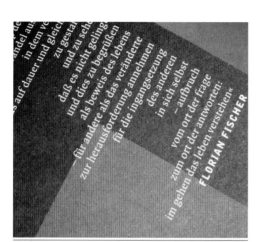

0342

0344

0343

0345

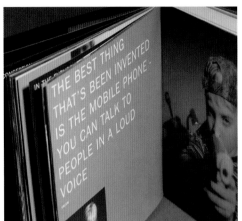

0346

0348

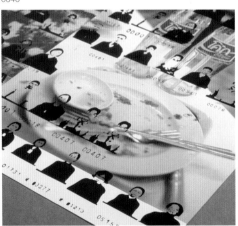

0347

0349

Editor-In-Chief	**Tom Loxley**
Art Director	**Ash Gibson**
Fashion Director	**Victoria Gaiger**
Fashion Forward Editor	**Nick Compton**
Editor At Large	**Bill Borrows**
Contributing Editor	**Greg Williams**

l Park: "the heyday of the margin".

critics, carping _in camera_ at errors and inconsistencies, private irritations that have only rarely found public expression in vitriolic ink. My usual complaint is against a lack of learning. Whilst pretentious comments likening the subject to other books ("If you enjoyed _The Dictionary of the Khazars_ [actually, rather a good book], then you'll love this") are, I find, seldom useful or accurate, they are rather fun. I like learning. I enjoy reading things by people who know what they're talking about. Worn lightly, learning assures you, the would-be reader, that there is some kind of value in what the reviewer has to say without alienating you with academic cant. In turn, a lack of learning (= downright ignorance) is insulting, invidious and cheap. (The reviewer who knows most about the book is, of course, the author himself, which this magazine has already realized.) My bibliophilic cards thus laid on the table, I hope you will take what I have to say to heart. _This_ review may just change your life.

By necessity, all reviews are subjective. But when did you last read one that actually reviewed the book itself? If you were going to buy a washing machine or a car, you might like to know what someone else thinks of it before getting out your wallet. For some reason, most reviewers seem to think that test-driving a book means simply passing on their comments on the text. They may as well be talking about some e-book aberration. Is that what you want? Of course not. You want a proper book, you want tactility, the expectant weight in your hand of paper and print as you take it home to read, the childishly simple enjoyment of opening a book for the first time. The object is important. Don't fall for the pulp Austen, its text smeared on to low-grade paper in an illegible type size, the whole crammed between pieces of glossy card with the actors in the latest TV adaptation smouldering from the cheesy cover, perhaps with

you drink champagne from a disposable plastic beaker?

To judge by the majority of modern reprints, the publisher's of a good edition is one where an introduction by some tinpot acac tells you what happens in the sto before you've had a chance to re it for yourself. If they must provi such padding, why don't they do sensible thing, like some Contine publishers, and furnish the book an afterword instead? It really m so much more sense ... Or, somet they offer you the original text, t literary version of recording Moz on period instruments, and invei you into buying it by audaciously branding it "the original edition" it isn't. They've missed the point experience, say, the original _Man Park_ as it appeared to the world 1814 (riddled as it was with error the text is just the start.

Austen's _Mansfield Park_ is a good example. The first thing tha strikes you about the original is that it is printed in three volume This effectively allows more than reader to use the book at the sam time, in a sort of staggered start. also looks elegant on the shelf. O a practical level, the division ma such a fat book more manageabl The reason for its substantiality becomes clear upon opening the This was the heyday of the marg 200 BC (Before Cost-cutting), Mc compositors please take note: rea like white space. The text is pres on a bed of white — the same m employed in restaurants that pre your meal to be set off appealing rather than piled up in a heap. Second, one notes the difference type size, line length and numbe of lines per page. The Germans do this today, their standard larg typefaces resulting in an easy ele and, it must be said, improved legibility. A quick comparison of first edition of _Mansfield Park_ wit the Penguin Classics reprint of 1

0352
emeryfrost
Australia

156/157

1000
Books +
mags.

THE DIY REVIEW

AN AUTHOR REVIEWS HIS OWN NEW BOOK

BURNING PARIS

Nicholas Blincoe
Sceptre, £16.99

First-time author James Beddoes's decision to write a history of the Siege of Paris and the subsequent revolutionary commune is a peculiar one. Nothing in Beddoes's background suggests a talent for fiction. He was completing a PhD in economics when he took a foreign posting with the World Bank, apparently to speed the break-up of his relationship with the mother of his young son. And suddenly … this, a full guns-blazing historical novel of love on the barricades.

I am deeply suspicious of the trend towards historical fiction. Any writer who

0353

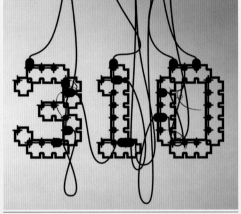

0355

0354

0356

0357
Non-Format
UK

158/159
1000
Books +
mags.

INTERVIEW

AN (UNFORTUNATE)
INTERVIEW WITH
HENRY
JAMES

BY CYNTHIA OZICK

Novelist and essayist Cynthia Ozick has been described as a 'narrative hypnotist' and one of the most important writers in America. Her first novel, *Trust*, was by her own admission heavily influenced by Henry James, and her obsession with his work hasn't exactly run dry. Appropriate, then, that she meets with him to set a few things straight

0359
emeryfrost
Australia

160/161

1000
Books +
mags.

BOB GELDOF
THE MAN WITH A PLAN

by Simon Finch, portrait by Nadav Kander

It was twenty years ago today Sergeant Pepper taught the band to play. Perhaps not, but it was twenty years ago that Geldof burst on to our television screens, furiously passionate and passionately furious. It was of course Live Aid, a massive global event focussed on simultaneous concerts on either side of the Atlantic. Footage of extreme human misery set against the savagely beautiful African scenery invaded our hot summer lives, invoking rightful shame and distress. Money poured in via telephone, bank draft and anonymous donation. In one particularly touching gesture, a group of Irish women donated their wedding rings; Bob was called and asked whether this gift should be accepted. He immediately replied, "Take the rings and keep hold of them for six weeks; if they come back, then give them back." They did not come back.

0360

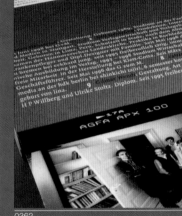

0362

0361

0363

0364
Untitled
UK

↘

162/163

1000
Books +
mags.

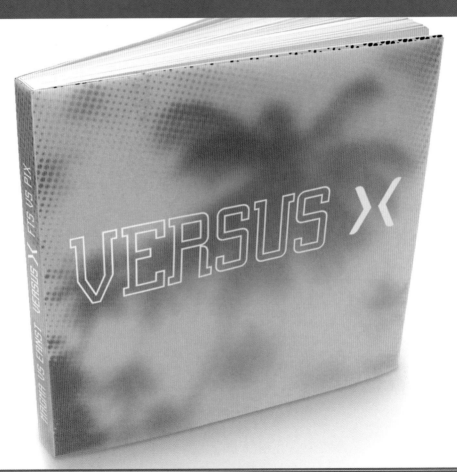

Ligalux GmbH
Germany

↘

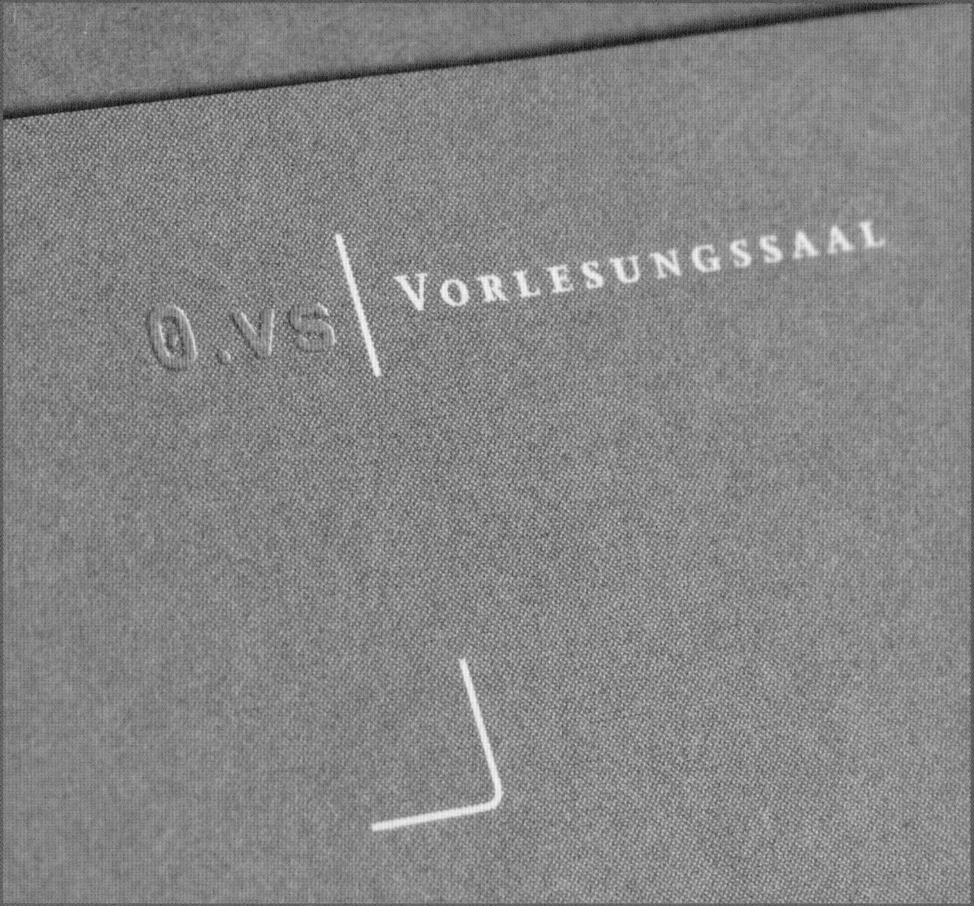

Chapter 3.
Logos + stationery.

Stationery
>

Logos

Brands

Compliment slips

Identities
>

Business cards

Letterheads

03 CAPOZZA

unreal
portable

brian eagle
creative director
12 Dyott St London WC1
20 7379 8752 M 077
eagle@unreal
real-uk.c

REACH EVEN
GREATER
HEIGHTS

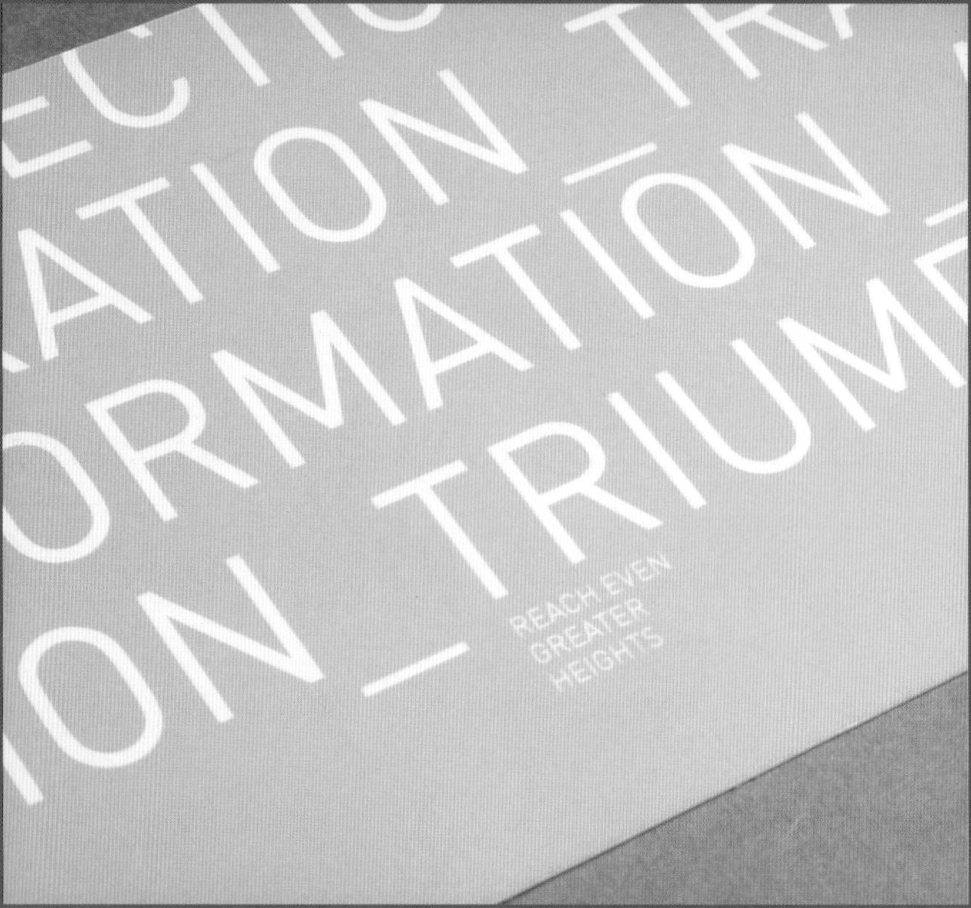

0368	0369	0370	0371	168/169

0368
Joe Miller's Company
USA
↘

0369
Hartford Design, Inc.
USA
↘↘

0370
Juicy Temples Creative
USA
↘

0371
Danielle Foushée Design
USA
↘↘

1000
Logos +
stationery

0368

0370

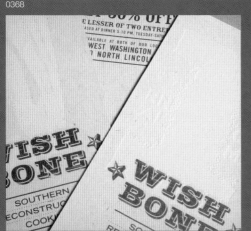

0369

0371

0372
Ph.D
USA
↘

0373
Yee-Ping Cho Design
USA
↘↘

0374
Ph.D
USA
↘

0375
Milton Glaser Inc.
USA
↘↘

0372

0374

0373

0375

0376

0378

0377

0379

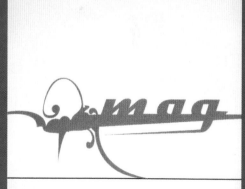

0381

Capsule
USA

↘

172/173

1000
Logos +
Stationery

0382
Wolken Communica
USA
↘

0383
Wolken Communica
USA
↘↘

0384
**The Family Design
International**
UK
↘

0385
Capaekel
UK
↘↘

0382

0384

0383

0385

0386	0387	0388	0389	174/175

0386
Segura Inc.
USA

0387
Si Scott
UK

0388
R&MAG Graphic Design
Italy

0389
Marino A. Gallo
USA

1000
Logos +
stationery

0386

0388

0387

0389

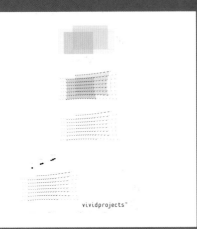

0390

0392

0391

0393

0394
**KearneyRocholl Corporate
Communications AG**
Germany

0395
**KearneyRocholl Corporate
Communications AG**
Germany

0396
Be Design
USA

0397
**The Family Design
International**
UK

176/177
1000
Logos +
stationery

0394

AREA ONE
AREA ONE

0395

0396

0397

0398
Harcus Design
Australia
↘

0399
Hoyne Design
Australia
↘↘

0400
elliottyoung
UK
↘

0401
Johann A. Gómez
USA
↘↘

ARINYA ACCESSORIES

0398

0400

OMVIVO

0399

wear®

0401

0402
Simon & Goetz Design
Germany

0403
Blok Design
Mexico

0404
Juicy Temples Creative
USA

0405
Segura Inc.
USA

178/179 | 1000 Logos + stationery

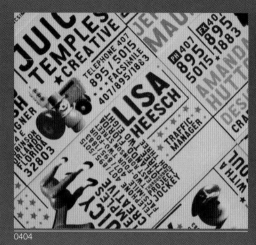

0402

0404

0403

0405

0406

0407

0408

0409

0410
Muggie Ramadani Design Studio
Denmark

180/181

1000
Logos +
stationery

0412
Yanek Iontef
Israel

182/183

1000
Logos +
stationery

0413
Rose Design
UK

0414
Academy of Art University
USA

0415
Segura Inc.
USA

0416
Planet 10
USA

0413

0415

SHE WILL CHANGE YOUR LIFE

0414

0416

0417
Si Scott
UK

184/185

1000
Logos +
stationery

0418

0420

0419

0421

0422
Stoecker Design
USA

0423
Ph.D
USA

0424
Q
Germany

0425
And Partners
USA

186/187

1000
Logos +
stationery

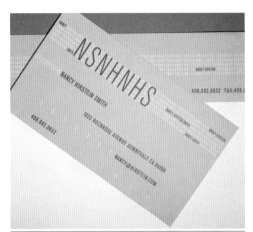

0422

0424

0423

0425

0427
R&MAG Graphic Design
Italy

0428
Starshot
Germany

0429
Vrontikis Design Office
USA

0430
Segura Inc.
USA

188/189

1000
Logos +
Stationery

0427

0429

0428

0430

0431

0432

0433

0434

0435
Liska & Associates, Inc.
USA

0436
Hornall Anderson Design Works, Inc.
USA

0437
Karim Rashid Inc.
USA

0438
**Muggie Ramadani
Design Studio**
Denmark

190/191

1000
Logos +
stationery

0435

0437

0436

0438

0439
The Family Design International
UK

0440
Ryan Burlinson
USA

0441
Karim Rashid Inc.
USA

0442
Joe Miller's Company
USA

0439

0441

0440

0442

(poetry center san josé)

0443
WilsonHarvey/Loewy
UK

192/193

1000
Logos +
stationery

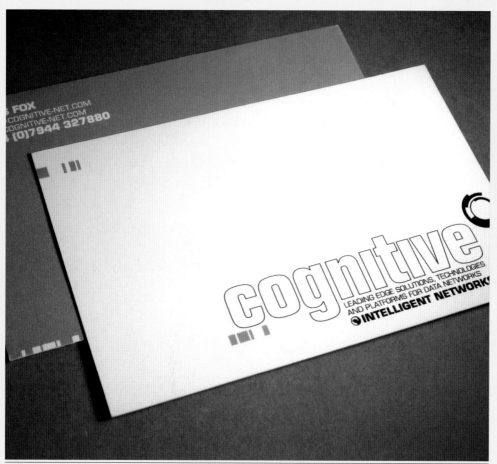

0445

0447

0446

0448

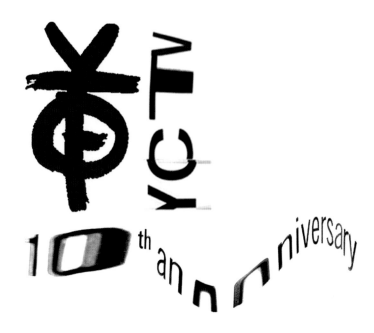

0453
Crush Design
UK
↘

0454
Crush Design
UK
↘↘

0455
Crush Design
UK
↘

0456
Crush Design
UK
↘↘

0453

0455

0454

0456

0457
Crush Design
UK
↘

0458
Crush Design
UK
↘↘

0459
Crush Design
UK
↘

0460
Crush Design
UK
↘↘

200/201 | 1000
Logos +
stationery

0457

0459

 ★Heineken|music **RELEASES ↓**

thirst

A MIX OF THE FRESHEST INGREDIENTS

FLY WITH
DESTINATION
HKN
GET ON BOARD

0462

0464

0463

0465

0466
**Muggie Ramadani
Design Studio**
Denmark

0467
**Muggie Ramadani
Design Studio**
Denmark

0468
**Muggie Ramadani
Design Studio**
Denmark

0469
Simon & Goetz Design
Germany

0466

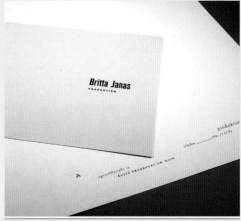

0468

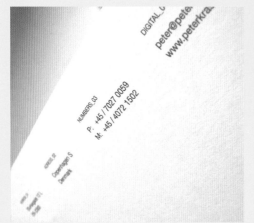

0467

0469

0470

Giorgio Davanzo Design
USA

204/205

1000
Logos +
stationery

0472
Ph.D
USA

206/207
1000
Logos +
stationery

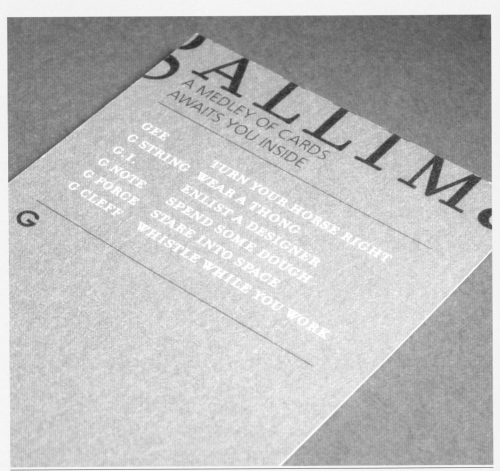

0474
Blok Design
Mexico

208/209

1000
Logos +
stationery

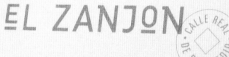

0475

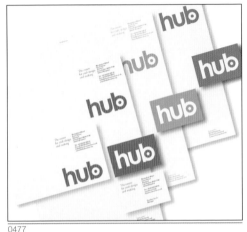

0477

0476

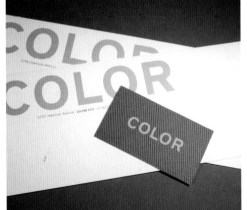

0478

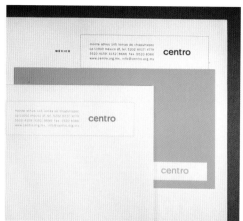

0479

0481

0480

0482

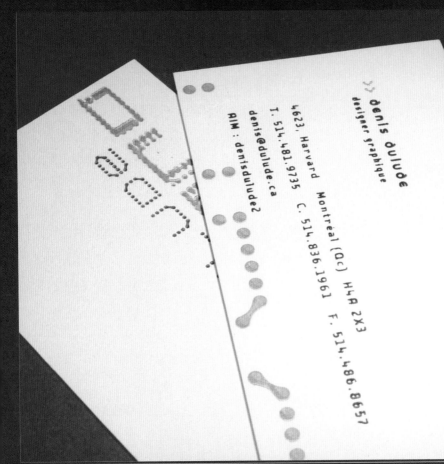

BASE

SMOOTH BASE
TYPE: WHITE/ REF NO. 034
BASEINTERIORS.COM

020 7487 3222
TEL. #

020 7487 3555
FAX. #

5 Oldbury Place
Marylebone Village
London W1U 5PE
OFFICE.

BASEINTERIORS.COM
SMOOTH BASE (120GSM) TYPE: WHITE/ REF

020 7487 32

TE

n W1U 5PE

0485

0487

0486

0488

0489	0490	0491	0492	214/215
WilsonHarvey/Loewy	**Unreal**	**Q**	**WilsonHarvey/Loewy**	1000 Logos + stationery
UK	UK	Germany	UK	

↘ ↘↘ ↘ ↘↘

0489

0491

0490

0492

>

Chapter 4.
Brochures.

>

—

Collateral

Annual reports
>

Product literature

Booklets

Pamphlets

Brochures
>

Folders

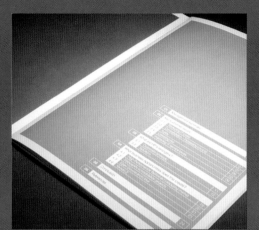

0494

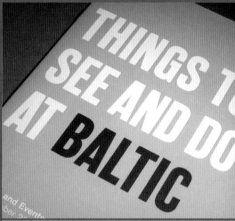

0496

0495

0497

0498

0500

0499

0501

0502
Anna B. Design
Germany

220/221
1000
Brochures

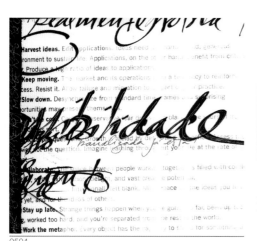

0504

0506

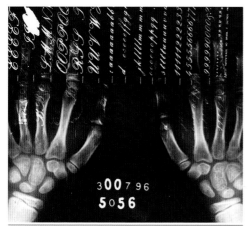

0505

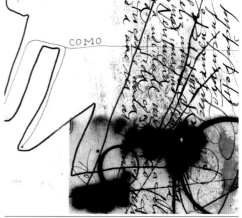

0507

0508

0510

0509

0511

0513
Simon & Goetz Design
Germany

0514
Simon & Goetz Design
Germany

0515
A2-GRAPHICS/SW/HK
UK

0516
Simon & Goetz Design
Germany

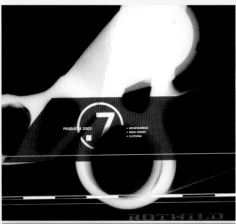

0513

0515

0514

0516

0517
Simon & Goetz Design
Germany

226/227

1000
Brochures

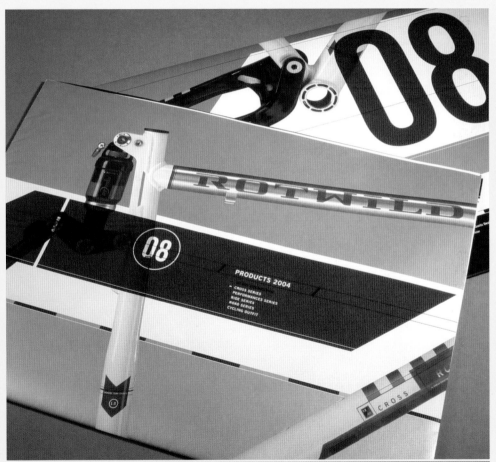

0518
Duffy Singapore
Singapore

0519
Dovetail Communications, Hartford Design, Woz Design
USA

0520
Cahan & Associates
USA

0521
Hartford Design, Inc.
USA

0518

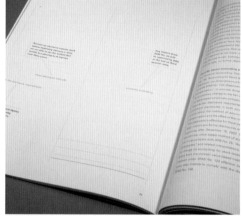

0520

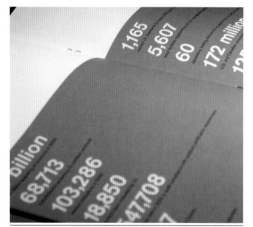

0519

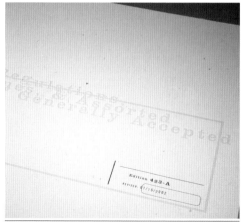

0521

0522
Hartford Design, Inc.
USA

0523
WilsonHarvey/Loewy
UK

0524
WilsonHarvey/Loewy
UK

0525
Joe Miller's Company
USA

228/229
1000 Brochures

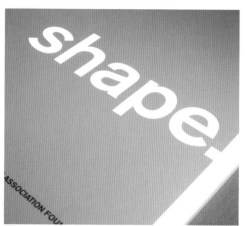

0522

0524

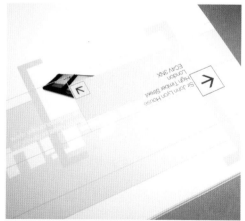

0523

0525

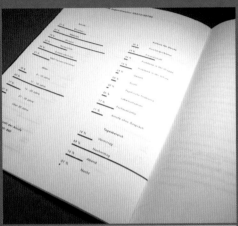

0526

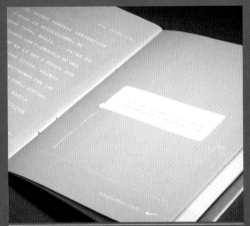

0528

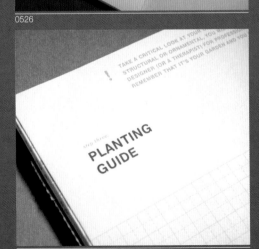

0527

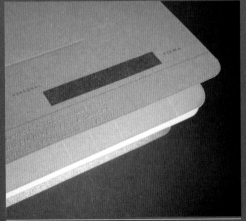

0529

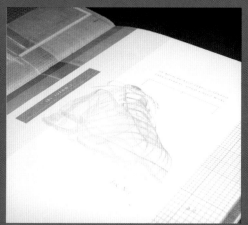

0530

0532

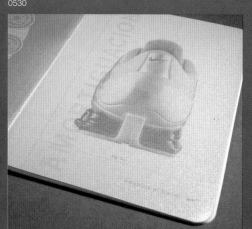

0531

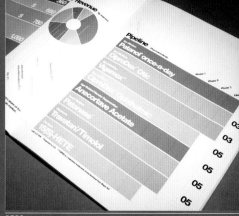

0533

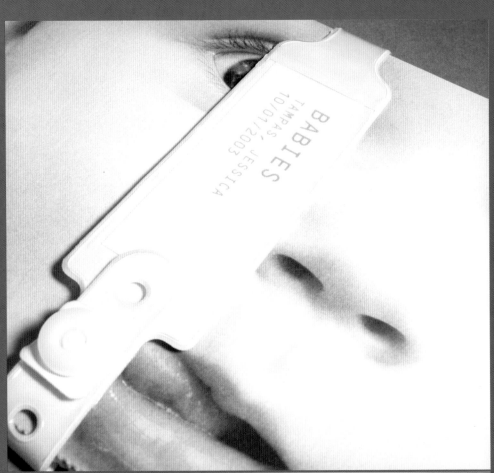

0535
Envision+
Germany
↘

232/233
1000
Brochures

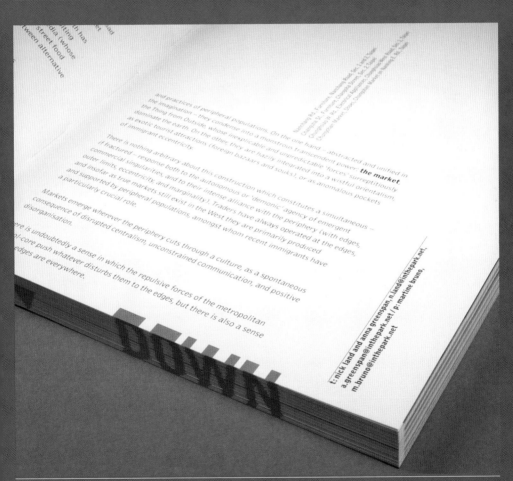

Nicola Bel S Furistan Standing Book Set set 5 for
Giorgino Sit. Furistan Changtji Stam Bell 5: Wan
Giorgino Sit. Furistan Karlingto Diplote Mei Wit
Giorgino Naïvé Spell Controan Meizor Mi Sutisct f m Van

and practices of peripheral populations. On the one hand – abstracted and unified in
the imagination – they condense into a monstrous transcendent power, **the market**,
the Thing from Outside, whose inexplicable and unpredictable 'forces' surreptitiously
dominate the earth. On the other they are hazily integrated into a wistful orientalism,
as exotic tourist attractions (foreign bazaars and souks), or as anomalous pockets
of immigrant eccentricity.

There is nothing arbitrary about this construction which constitutes a simultaneous –
if fractured – response both to the autonomous or 'demonic' agency of emergent
commercial singularities, and to their intense alliance with the periphery (with edges,
outer limits, eccentricity, and marginality). Traders have always operated at the edges,
and insofar as true markets still exist in the West they are primarily produced
and supported by peripheral populations, amongst whom recent immigrants have
a particularly crucial role.

Markets emerge wherever the periphery cuts through a culture, as a spontaneous
consequence of disrupted centralism, unconstrained communication, and positive
disorganisation.

[th]ere is undoubtedly a sense in which the repulsive forces of the metropolitan
[contr]ol-core push whatever disturbs them to the edges, but there is also a sense
[in which] edges are everywhere.

t: nick land and anna greenspan n.land@inthepark.net,
a.greenspan@inthepark.net / p: martine bruno,
m.bruno@inthepark.net

0536

0537

0538

0539

0540
Envision+
Germany

234/235
1000
Brochures

sean milborne, jewellery designer and gemologist, wears coat by rollo research, top by kenx and scarf by tim ryan. ∗ orla highland, producer, wears matching.

abhair gnó
talking business

monn mcloughlin

0542 | 0543
Dulude | **Dulude**
Canada | Canada
↘ | ↘↘

0544 | 0545 | 236/237
Dulude | **Dulude** | 1000 Brochures
Canada | Canada
↘ | ↘↘

0542

0543

0544

0545

0546

0548

0547

0549

0550

0552

0551

0553

0554   0555
Untitled **Untitled**
UK   UK
↘   ↘↘

0556   0557
Untitled **Untitled**
UK   UK
↘   ↘↘

0554

0556

0555

0557

0558
Cahan & Associates
USA

0559
Cahan & Associates
USA

0560
Cahan & Associates
USA

0561
Cahan & Associates
USA

240/241
1000
Brochures

0558

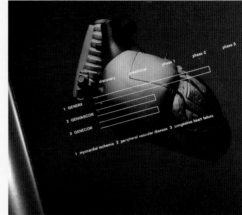

0560

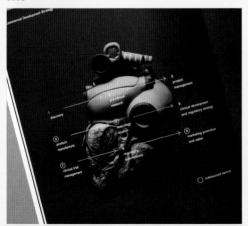

0559

0561

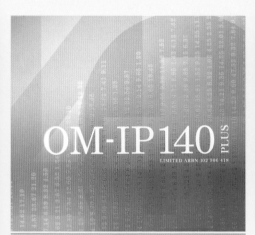

0563

0565

0564

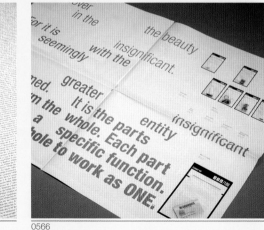

0566

0568
Hornall Anderson Design Works, Inc.
USA
↘

0569
Hornall Anderson Design Works, Inc.
USA
↘↘

0570
Hornall Anderson Design Works, Inc.
USA
↘

0571
Hornall Anderson Design Works, Inc.
USA
↘↘

244/245
1000 Brochures

0568

0570

0569

0571

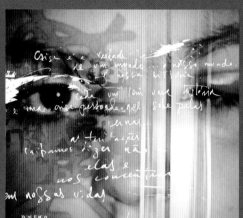

0572

0574

0573

0575

0576

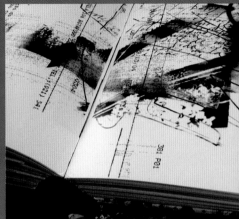

0578

0577

0579

Ballymena
os project in Ballymena puts mobility and biodiversity into action, actual habitats developed to increase water and diversity of plant and animal s in the area. The flush building uses panels, wind turbines and renewable eds act as a natural filtration system rify waste water.

25
Strangford Stone/
Killyleagh

28
Groundwork's
Changing Places

10
National Paralife/
Newcastle

25
Millennium Greens

Blaenffordd Ffyriol/Snowdonia

64
After decades of neglect, a 40km section of the Welsh highland railway is being reconstructed, running from Caernarfon to Porthmadog. Due for completion in 2009, steam and diesel locomotives will climb through the Snowdonia National Park, offering passengers breathtaking views.

11
Parc Betwebwl/
Denali coast

Canolfan Mileniwm/Cardiff

47
Providing a focus for Welsh culture, identity and talent is the Wales Millennium Centre on the Cardiff Bay waterfront. Musically, opera and dance will be staged in a resurrected building forged from porous materials – including slate blocks from north Wales and fossilized tree ferns from the coal measures of South Wales.

Wildscreen at-Bristol

33
Wildscreen at-Bristol brings up-to-date computer and video technology to explain our natural world. A walk-through botanical house with free-flying birds and butterflies and a giant IMAX cinema enable visitors to watch nature at an incredible scale. Wildscreen's ARKive – a digital zoo – is a globally-accessible collection of natural history films, photographs and sound recordings.

42
Church Floodlighting

Eden Project/St Austell

30
Visitors to the Eden Project in Cornwall have the opportunity to experience some of the world's most dramatic and useful plants at first hand, with two enormous 'biomes' (greenhouses) exhibiting plants from four climates – rainforest, mediterranean, desert and temperate. The project targets the relationship between people, plants and resources – and how this must be managed to improve sustainability.

The Lowry/Salford

20
Salford Quays – at the heart of Manchester's waterways – plays host to The Lowry, a powerhouse for the performing and visual arts. Home to the world's largest collection of works by local artist LS Lowry, the centre also boasts exhibition spaces for visiting collections, plus two theatres.

17
Greencia/
Stoke-on-Trent

55
Millennium Point/
Birmingham

St Edmundsbury Cathedral

44
For nearly 1000 years the site of the cathedral in Bury St Edmunds, Suffolk, has been a place of worship and pilgrimage. The construction of today's cathedral was started in 1503, yet remained unfinished, and the current project focuses on the completion of the North Transept, the Cloisters and the dramatic Central Tower.

61
National Space
Centre/Leicester

83
Torrs Walkway/
New Mills

Portsmouth Harbour

52
This historic maritime centre is being given a new waterfront. At the heart of the development is the impressive sail-like structure of the Tide Spinnaker Tower which will provide visitors with an unparalleled view of the Mary Rose and HMS Victory – potent reminders of the port's seafaring history.

19
North Sea

29
Trees for The
Millennium

Nile End Park/London

23
The redevelopment and restoration of Mile End park in London's East End has been achieved through active cooperation with local residents. Community planning sessions highlighted the need for recreational facilities combined with environmental initiatives, and features include a swimming pool and athletics track, plus ecology and children's centres, gallery spaces, cafés and a concert stadium.

18
Tate Modern/London

08
Lighting Croydon's
skyline

31
Millennium
Sound Booth/
Hartlepic

14
Work of Life/
London Zoo

24
Norfolk and Norwich
Project

26
Trans Pennine Trail

15
Earth Centre/Doncaster

14
Project
107V/Teesside

57
Body/The Dome

0581
**Lippa Pearce Design,
London**
UK
↘

0582
**Lippa Pearce Design,
London**
UK
↘↘

0583
**Lippa Pearce Design,
London**
UK
↘

0584
**Lippa Pearce Design,
London**
UK
↘↘

248/249 | 1000 Brochures

Graphic designers Why Not Associates have, in
collaboration with artist Gordon Young, created
'A Flock of Words' to celebrate the bird watching haven
of Morecambe Bay on the north west coast of England.

The 320m long typographic pavement is constructed
from granite, concrete, steel, brass, bronze and glass,
and was officially opened to the public on 6 June 2003.
It is a truly unique project that has all the creatives
and manufacturers involved exploring the boundaries
of their specialisations.

0581

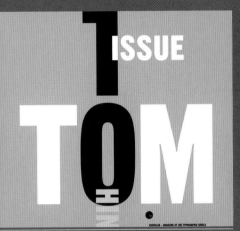

0583

0582

0584

The design firm House Industries was founded in Wilmington, Delaware in 1993 by partners Andy Cruz and Rich Roat. In their illustrious and epic ten-year career, they have mastered a large cross-section of design disciplines. From their early forays into distressed digital type to their recent collaborations with acclaimed architects Richard and Dion Neutra and pop artist Shag, House Industries refuses to be bound by narrow definitions of 'graphic design.'

Known internationally as a prolific type foundry, House has forever changed the design world. Their unique type products can be seen anywhere from your favourite brand of cereal to highly circulated magazines and television shows. House fonts have become essential tools no designer can live without.

Their font and design work deftly melds cultural, musical and graphical elements. In a recent article about House Industries in *Juxtapoz* magazine, Sven Kirsten writes, 'They are good at what they do because they not only appreciate art, aesthetics and style but are also in love with concepts. Their font kits are microcosms of the pop culture they represent. Their products are not just fonts; they're a lifestyle.'

In the past couple of years, House has taken their complete 'lifestyle' approach to designing fonts to a new level. In 1999, *House Magazine* was launched to journal the details and inspiration of House Industries' creative process. The firm then topped themselves by developing a successful textile line that is the initial foray into a range of home accessories.

House still has plenty up their sleeves. The recently released Neutra Boomerang chair marks the beginning of furniture production, while their partnership with Nano Universe (Japan) has them dabbling in the world of fashion. A ten-year retrospective book featuring their work will be published in spring 2004.

B1LL
CAHAN
ISSUE 0

CIRCULAR – MAGAZINE OF THE TYPOGRAPHIC CIRCLE

Issue 10 featuring Tom Hingston, Bill Cahan and Hans Schleger.

£10 plus £2 p&p. For further information on either Circular or

All models, tecnical data, performances,
photos, tecnical drawings etc are displayed

Manufacturer: Belgian Motors
Model: Storm IV Twin Pod Cloud Car
CrW: 2 being
Max. speed: 1.500km/h
Engines: Quadex Kyronaster ion engine
Armament: 2 blaster cannons
Power: Incom Corporation T-r-2 generator

ALTERNATOR (3x400/230 volts, 50 Hz, 1500 rpm.)

engine

chassis

0588	0589	0590	0591	252/253

Lippa Pearce Design, London
UK

Guru Design
Denmark

Guru Design
Denmark

Metal
USA

1000 Brochures

0588

0590

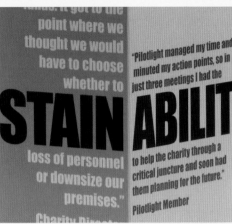

0589

0591

0592

0594

0593

0595

0596
Enspace, Inc.
USA

254/255

1000
Brochures

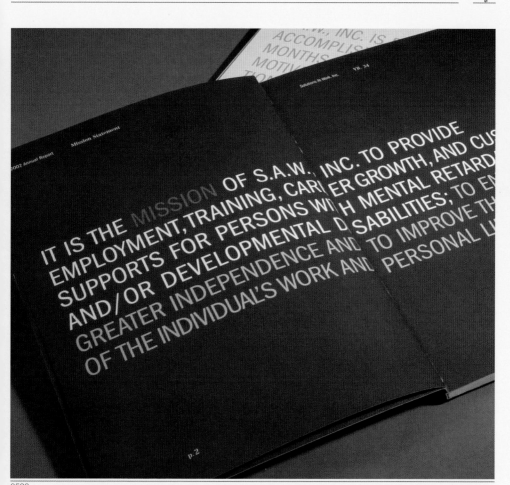

Neutro-
penia

Operand
G-CSF
for the treatment
of neutropenia

Neutropenia is a severe decrease in neutrophil cell counts in the blood. Neutrophils are a specific type of blood cell that play an important role in the human body's defense against bacterial infections. Neutropenia is a common side effect from chemotherapeutic treatments of many forms of cancer, including breast cancer, lung cancer, lymphomas and leukemias. Neutropenic patients contract bacterial infections easily and often, some of which can be severe and life-threatening. Further, neutropenic patients may receive reduced or delayed chemotherapy treatment, which can result in disease progression.

0598
A2-GRAPHICS/SW/HK
UK
↘

0599
Bruketa & Zinić
Croatia
↘↘

0600
A2-GRAPHICS/SW/HK
UK
↘

0601
Bruketa & Zinić
Croatia
↘↘

256/257
:1000
Brochures

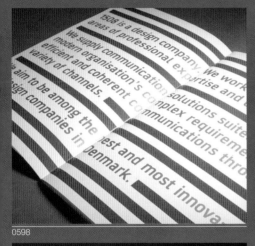

0598

0600

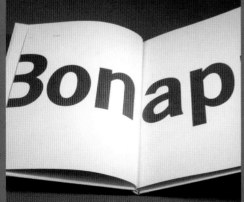

0599

0601

0602

0604

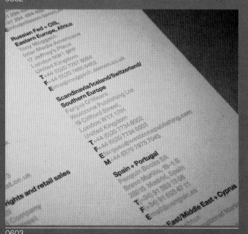

0603

0605

0606
Phyx Design
USA

0607
Blue River
UK

0608
Twelve: Ten
UK

0609
Twelve: Ten
UK

258/259
1000 Brochures

0606

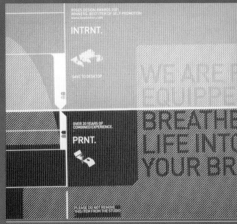

0608

0607

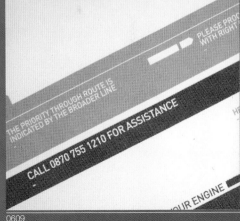

0609

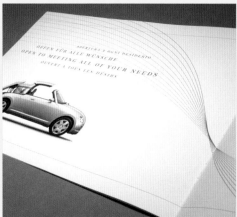

0610

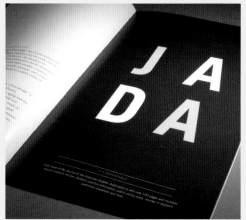

0612

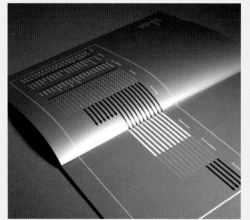

0611

0613

0614
Pangaro Beer
USA

260/261

1000
Brochures

0616
Duffy Singapore
Singapore

262/263

1000
Brochures

0618
Guru Design
Denmark

0619
Harcus Design
Australia

0620
**Muggie Ramadani
Design Studio**
Denmark

0621
Guru Design
Denmark

264/265
:1000
Brochures

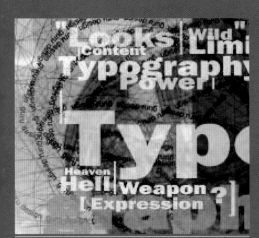

0618

0620

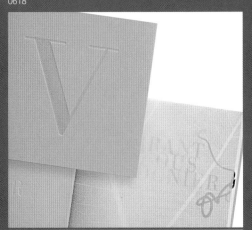

0619

0621

0622
Cahan & Associates
USA
↘

0623
Cahan & Associates
USA
↘↘

0624
Cahan & Associates
USA
↘

0625
**Muggie Ramadani
Design Studio**
Denmark
↘↘

0622

0624

0623

0625

0626
344 Design, LLC
USA
↘

0627
**Design Depot
Creative Bureau**
Russia
↘↘

0628
**Design Depot
Creative Bureau**
Russia
↘

0629
**Design Depot
Creative Bureau**
Russia
↘↘

266/267
1000 Brochures

0626

0627

0629

0631

0633

0632

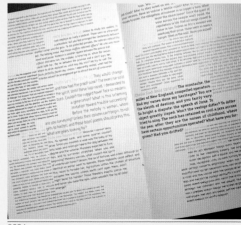

0634

0635

0637

0636

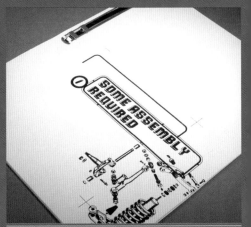

0638

0639	0640		0641	0642	270/271

0639 WilsonHarvey/Loewy UK ↘

0640 Monster Design USA ↘↘

0641 Segura Inc USA ↘

0642 WilsonHarvey/Loewy UK ↘↘

1000 Brochures

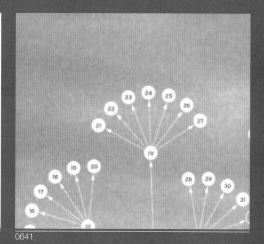

0639

0641

0640

0642

0643

0644

ICB.
PUTTING SERVICE
FIRST.

0645

2004 has been exclusively developed for Chief Financial Officers and Chief Information Officers operating in leading blue chip organisations across Europe. Use this seminar to align your IT and Finance functions and improve the long term performance of your organisation. Places are limited and are only available to invited delegates. Register immediately using the enclosed fastback form or contact our registration hotline on 020 7420 7700 to secure your place at the summit.

WHY ATTEND:
THE INFORMATION FOR PROFI
SUMMIT 2004 OFFERS A STRA
HIGH VALUE AGENDA TO HELP
REALISE THE VALUE OF YOUR
ENTERPRISE-WIDE. OUR PANE
SPEAKERS HAS BEEN SELECT
OFFER INSIGHT AND PRACTIC
ADVICE TO HELP YOU CONVER
INFORMATION INTO HARD CUR
COMBINING STRATEGIC CONS
CASE EXPERIENCE AND TECHN
ADVICE. THIS SEMINAR WILL
YOU RE-EVALUATE YOUR ORGA
TIONS STRATEGIC DECISION-
PROCESSES FOR IMPROVED R
GROWTH AND A GREATER RET
YOUR ASSETS.

INFORMATION FOR PROFIT 2004:
THE INFORMATION FOR PROFIT SUMMIT 2004 IS AN EXCLUSIVE BREAK
FAST BRIEFING FOR EXECUTIVES LOOKING TO ACHIEVE COMPETITIVE
ADVANTAGE THROUGH IMPROVED INFORMATION MANAGEMENT AND
DECISION-MAKING. SCHEDULED FOR THE 25TH FEBRUARY, THIS EVENT
HAS BEEN SPECIALLY FORMULATED BY LEADING SOLUTION PROVIDER

0646

0647
AdamsMorioka, Inc.
USA
↘

0648
Wonksite
Colombia
↘↘

0649
Underware
The Netherlands
↘

0650
Wonksite
Colombia
↘↘

272/273

1000 Brochures

0647

0649

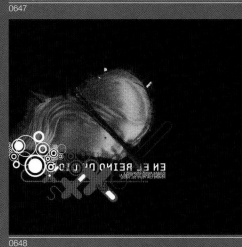

0648

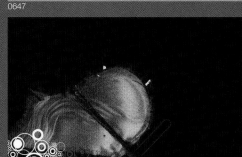

0650

0652
Voice
Australia

274/275
1000
Brochures

print media / session styling

pr   m ia /

print media / session styling

prin t m edia
sess ion styl i ng

SECTION

0654
Cahan & Associates
USA
↘

0655
Cahan & Associates
USA
↘↘

0656
SalterBaxter
UK
↘

0657
Motive Design Research
USA
↘↘

276/277
1000
Brochures

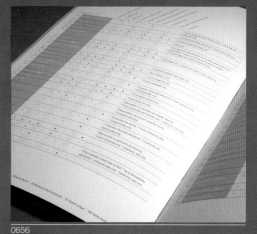

0654

0656

0655

0657

0658

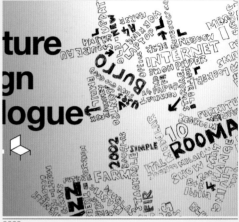

0660

0659

0661

0662

BBK Studio
USA

278/279

1000
Brochures

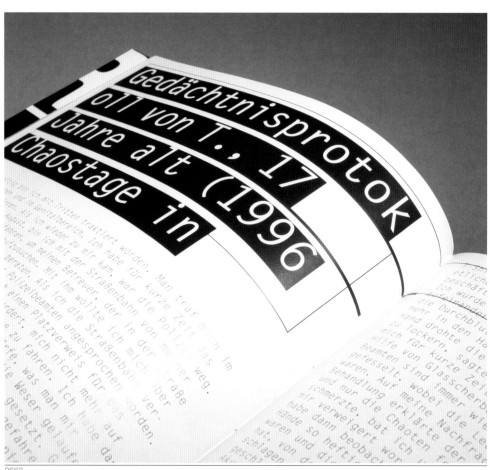

0664

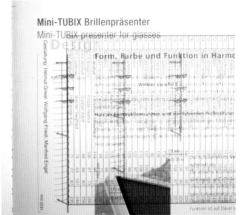

0666

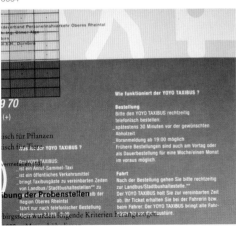

0665

0667

0668

0670

0669

0671

0672
Sommese Design
USA

282/283

1000
Brochures

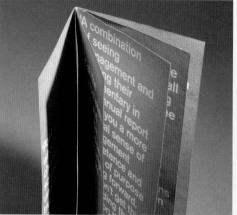

0673

0675

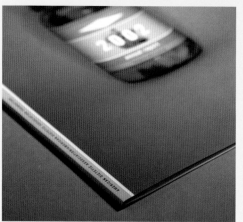

0674

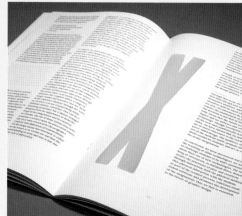

0676

'...g and ...etely ...bling manner.'

...eporting
I don't
...rsonally,
...ve to
...and
...s it

Fund Manager

...mpany, not th...
brokers' notes.'

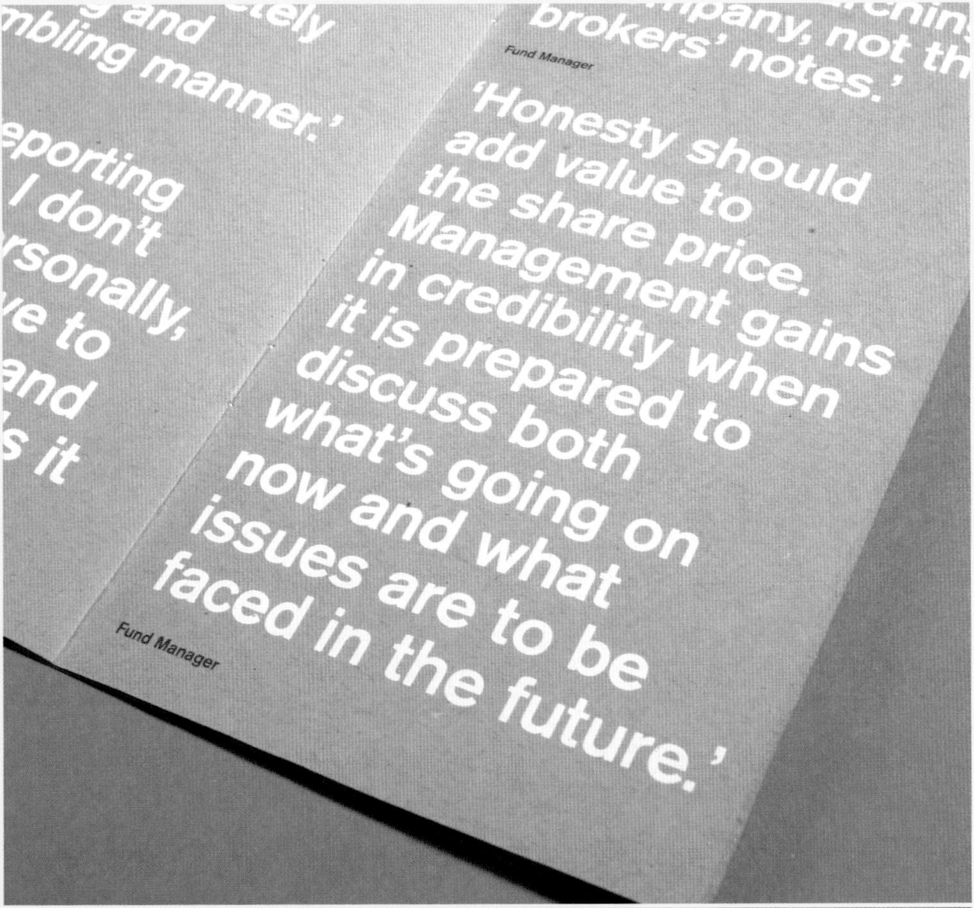

Fund Manager

'Honesty should
add value to
the share price.
Management gains
in credibility when
it is prepared to
discuss both
what's going on
now and what
issues are to be
faced in the future.'

Dulude
Canada

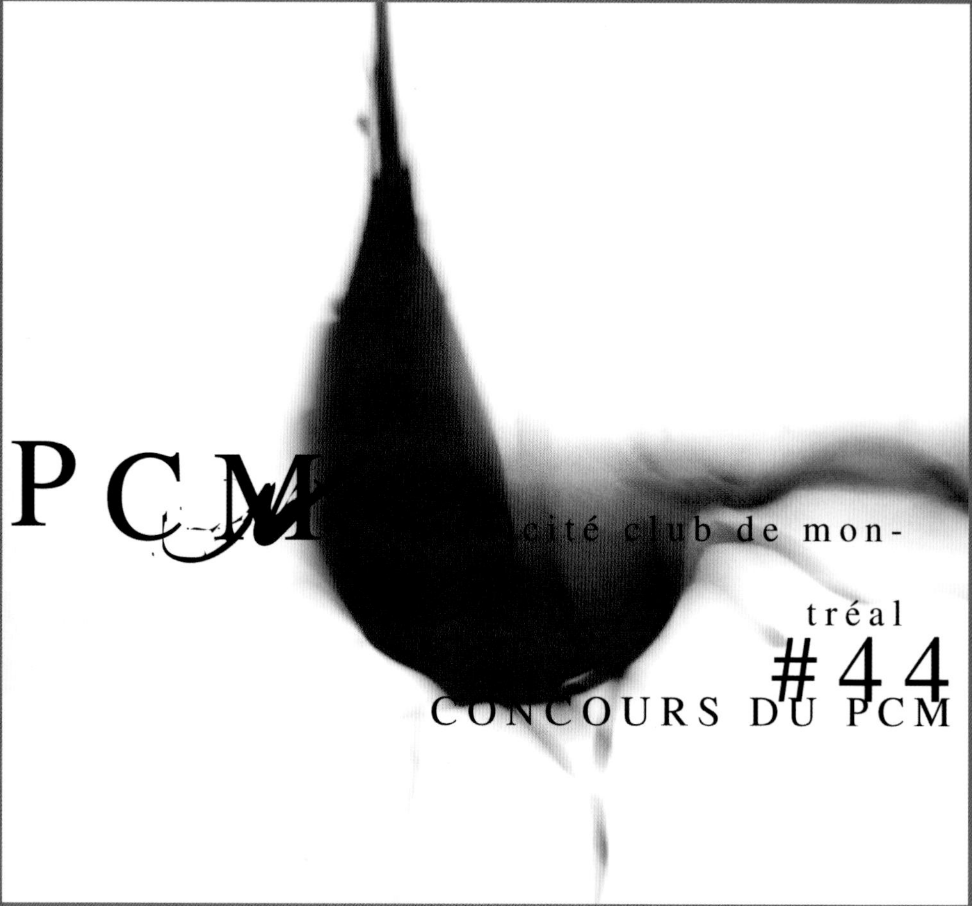

0679 Ligalux GmbH Germany

0680 Ligalux GmbH Germany

0681 Ligalux GmbH Germany

0682 Ligalux GmbH Germany

286/287
1000 Brochures

0679

0681

0680

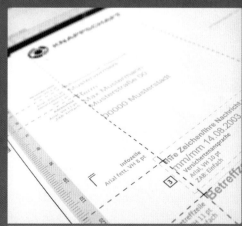

0682

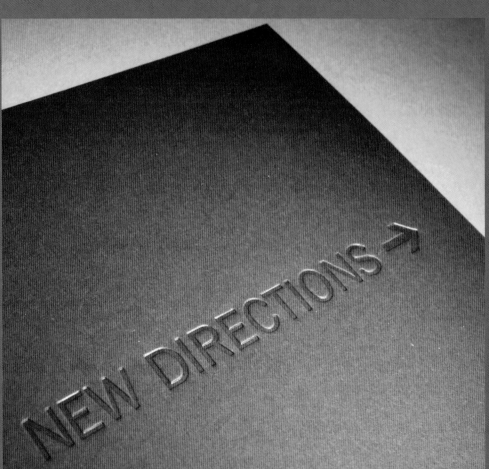

0684
KROG
Slovenia

288/289
1000
Brochures

0685
Underware
The Netherlands
↘

0686
Metal
USA
↘↘

0687
The Family Design International
UK
↘

0688
And Partners
USA
↘↘

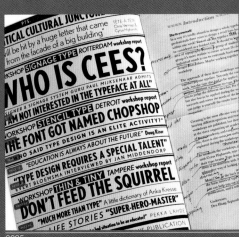

0685

0687

0686

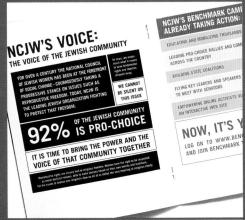

0688

0689
Capsule
USA

↘

290/291
1000
Brochures

0691

YOUR VOICE. IT'S TIME TO SPEAK OUT AND FIGHT BACK. ON JANUARY 22, 1973 THE SUPREME COURT AFFIRMED WOMEN'S CONSTITUTIONAL RIGHT TO ABORTION IN ITS LANDMARK *ROE V. WADE* RULING. TODAY THIS RIGHT IS UNDER ATTACK IN COURTROOMS ACROSS THE COUNTRY. YOU CAN DO SOMETHING ABOUT IT. TAKE ACTION TODAY, BEFORE IT'S TOO LATE.

0693

0692

0694

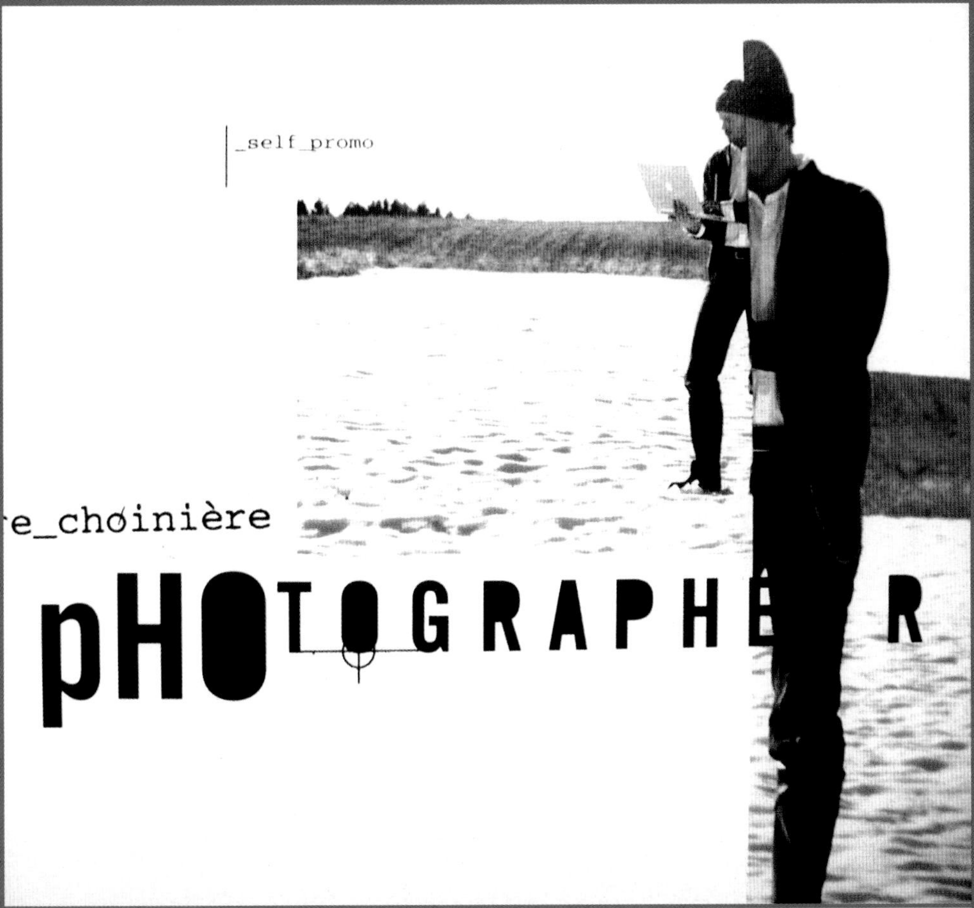

_self_promo

re_choinière

pHOTOGRAPHER

0697
Ligalux GmbH
Germany

0698
Ligalux GmbH
Germany

0699
Ligalux GmbH
Germany

0700
Ligalux GmbH
Germany

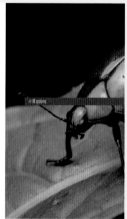

0697

0699

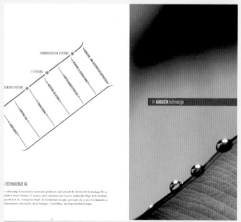

0698

0700

0701

0703

0702

0704

Twelve: Ten
UK

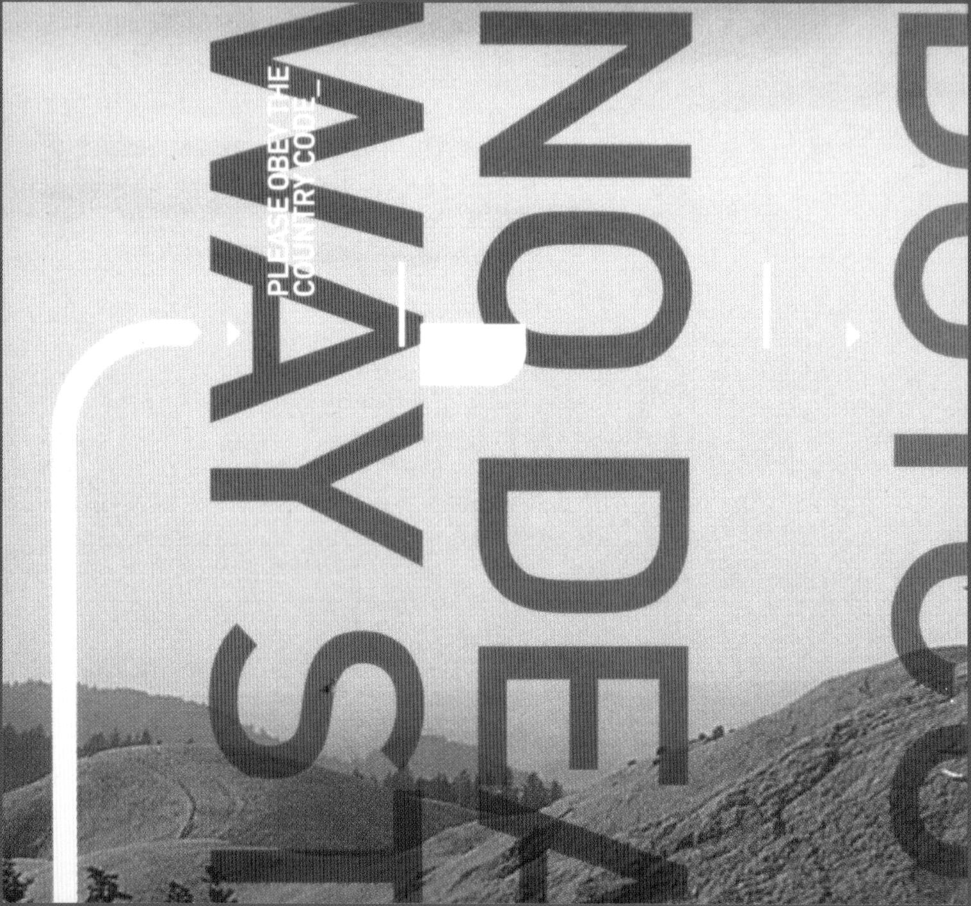

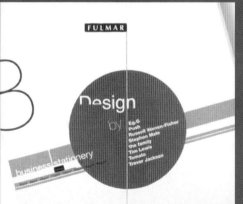

0706

0708

0707

0709

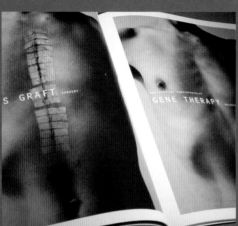

0710

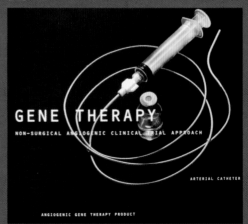

0712

0711

0713

0714

0716

0715

0717

0719
**KearneyRocholl Corporate
Communications AG**
Germany

0720
**KearneyRocholl Corporate
Communications AG**
Germany

0721
**KearneyRocholl Corporate
Communications AG**
Germany

0722
**KearneyRocholl Corporate
Communications AG**
Germany

302/303

1000 Brochures

0719

0721

0720

0722

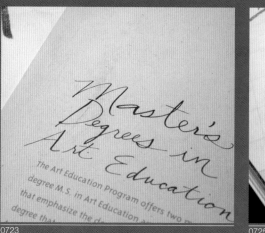

0723

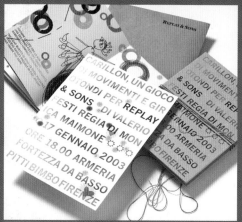

0724

0725

0726

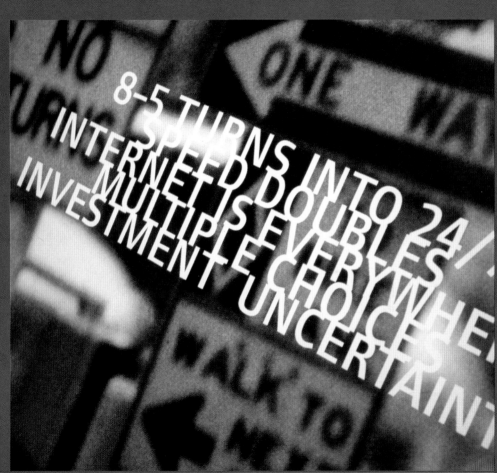

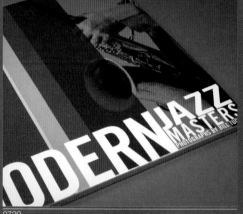

0729

0731

0730

0732

0733
Strichpunkt
Germany

0734
Strichpunkt
Germany

0735
AdamsMorioka, Inc.
USA

0736
Eggers & Diaper
Germany

0733

0734

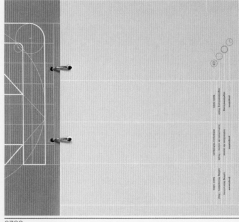

0736

0735

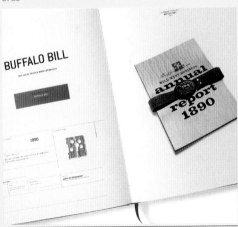

0737

0739

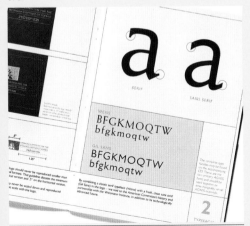

0738

0740

{ CONTENTS }
*

04
A NOTE FROM THE CHANCELLOR

05
FORWARD
Dr. Annette Stott
Director, School of Art and Art History

07
MULTICULTURALISM: **THE SEARCH FOR** ETHNIC, SEXUAL AND
RACIAL **IDENTITY IN A POSTMODERN WORLD**
Kent Logan

11
ROBERT COLESCOTT & **GLENN LIGON** * CONFRONTING **CARICATURE** &
STEREOTYPE
Dr. Shannen Hill
Director, Victoria H. Myhren Gallery

20
PLATES

30
ARTIST BIOGRAPHIES: ROBERT COLESCOTT, GLENN LIGON

32
WORKS IN THE EXHIBITION

*

plied by Vicki and Kent Logan and are repro
mission of the artists or their representatives

. Plates 1-2, Phyllis Kind Gallery;
io Terras Gallery.

& Warinner
inator: Celeste McMullin, the Printcess

ROBERT**COLESCOTT**&
&GLENNLIGON

FROM THE **LOGAN** COLLECTION

UNIVERSITY OF DENVER
VICTORIA H. MYHREN GALLERY

JANUARY 9–FEBRUARY 27

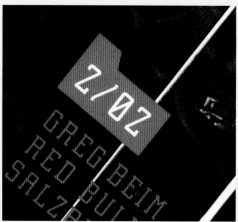

0743

0745

0744

0746

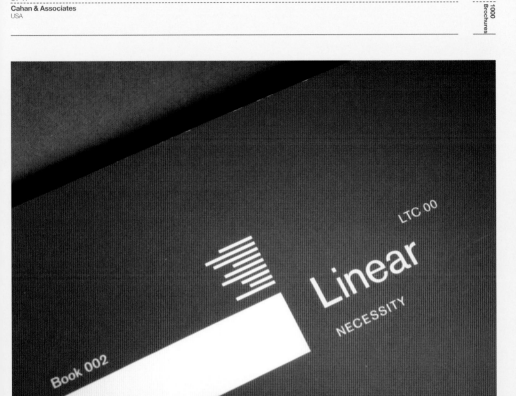

Chapter 5.
Posters + banners.

Posters
>

Banners
>

PRETTY
GIRLS

MAKE GRAVES.

SMALL BROWN BIKE
BREAKING PANGEA
THURSDAY MARCH SEVENTH
FIRST UNITARIAN CHURCH

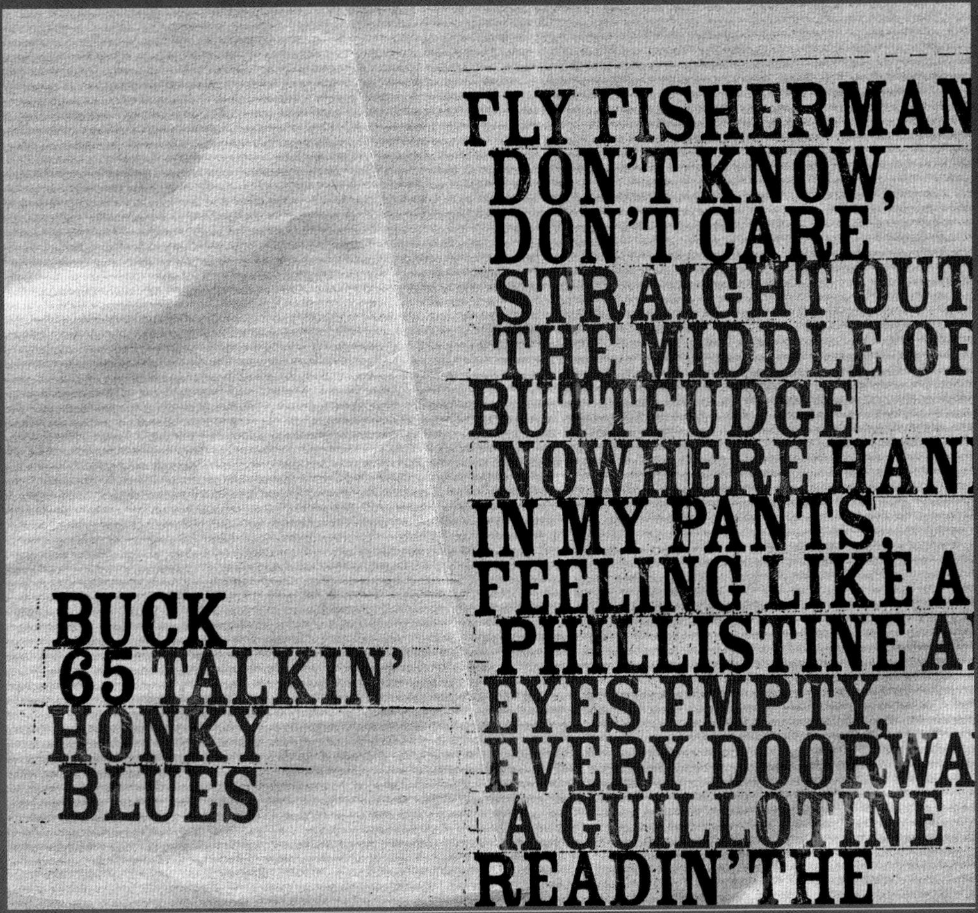

FLY FISHERMAN
DON'T KNOW,
DON'T CARE
STRAIGHT OUT
THE MIDDLE OF
BUTTFUDGE
NOWHERE HAN
IN MY PANTS,
FEELING LIKE A
PHILLISTINE A
EYES EMPTY,
EVERY DOORWA
A GUILLOTINE
READIN' THE

BUCK
65 TALKIN'
HONKY
BLUES

0750

0752

0751

0753

0754
Beautiful
UK

0755
Beautiful
UK

0756
Beautiful
UK

0757
Beautiful
UK

318/319 | 1000 Posters + banners

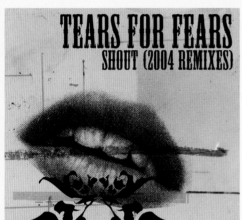

0754

0756

0755

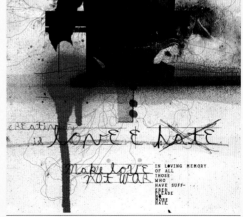

0757

0759
Segura Inc.
USA

320/321

1000
Posters +
banners

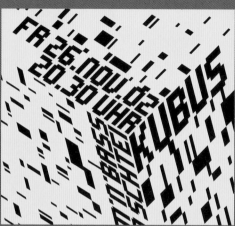

0760

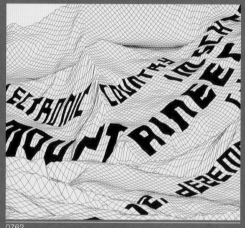

0762

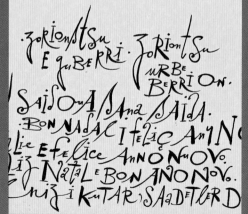

0761

0763

0764	0765	0766	0767	322/323
Polite Design Incorporated	**Cheng Design**	**NB:Studio**	**Cheng Design**	1000 Posters + banners
USA	USA	UK	USA	

↘   ↘↘   ↘   ↘↘

0764

0766

0765

0767

AUX CÔTÉS DES TOMATO, ET A ÉGALEMENT ENSEIGNE LA TYPOGRAPHIE À L'UNIVERSITÉ DU QUÉBEC À MONTRÉAL.
POUR SON STYLE GRAPHIQUE HORS-NORMES, IL A ÉTÉ INVITÉ À DONNER DES CONFÉRENCES EN EUROPE AUX CÔTÉS DES TOMATO, FELLA ET BRODY, ET A ÉGALEMENT ENSEIGNE LA TYPOGRAPHIE À L'UNIV
IATEUR DE LA PREMIÈRE TYPOTHÈQUE AU QUÉBEC, 2REBELS, IL S'EST RAPIDEMENT FAIT CONNAÎTRE POUR SON STYLE GRAPHIQUE HORS-NORMES. IL A ÉTÉ INVITÉ À DONNER DES CONFÉRENCES EN EUROP
T LE MONDE DU SPECTACLE, DENIS A ENTAMÉ UNE CARRIÈRE DE DESIGNER GRAPHIQUE EN FORCE : INSTIGATEUR DE LA PREMIÈRE TYPOTHÈQUE AU QUÉBEC, 2REBELS, IL S'EST RAPIDEMENT FAIT CONNAÎT

mardi 16 septembre 2003

Usine C

0771

0773

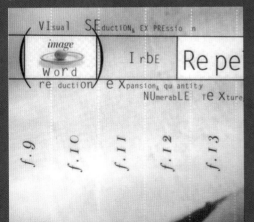

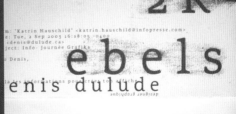

0772

0774

0775	0776
A3 Design	**Harrimansteel**
USA	UK
↘	↘↘

0777	0778
Wolken Communica	**IAAH/iamalwayshungry**
USA	USA
↘	↘↘

0775

0777

0776

0778

0779

0781

0780

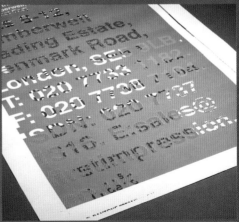

0782

0783

0785

0784

0786

0787
**Lippa Pearce Design,
London**
UK

0788
344 Design, LLC
USA

0789
Yanek Iontef
Israel

0790
**Lippa Pearce Design,
London**
UK

330/331

1000
Posters +
banners

0787

0789

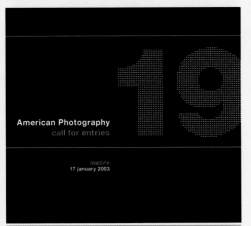

0788

0790

Juan Torneros
Colombia

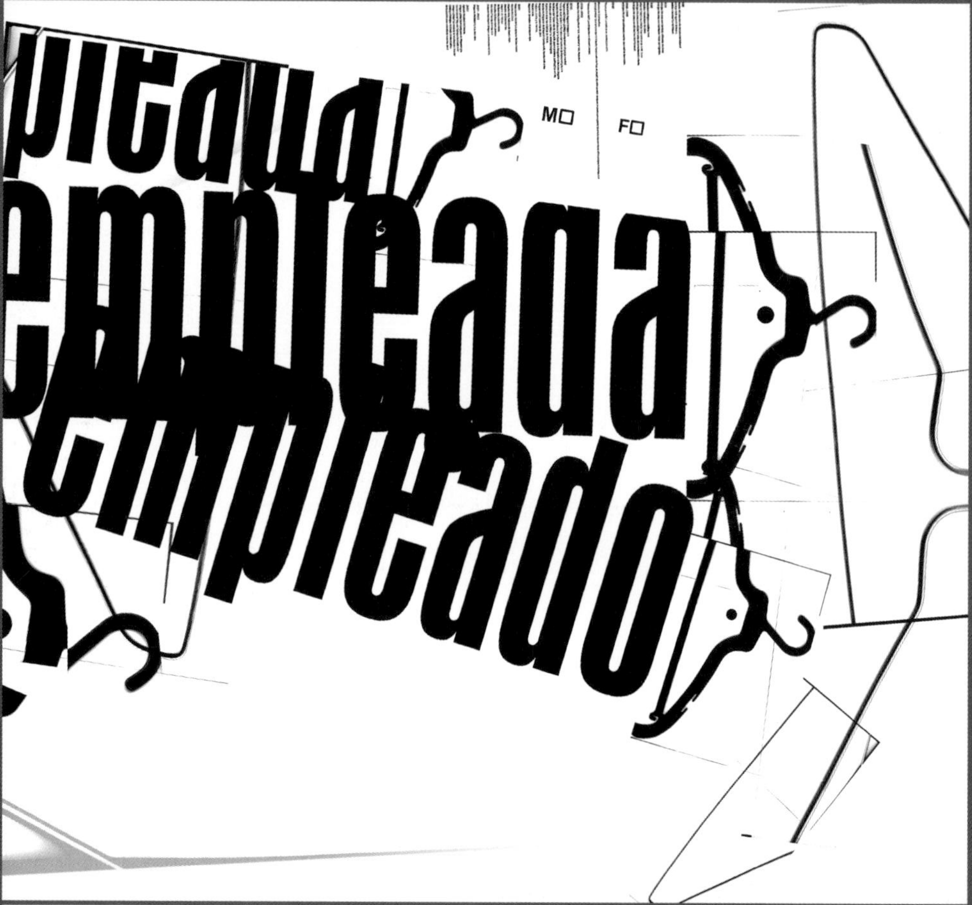

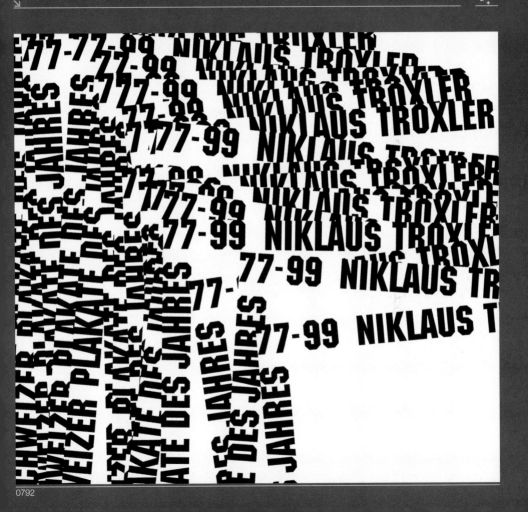

0793

0795

0794

0796

0797

Gervais
The Netherlands

↘

334/335

1000
Posters +
banners

0799

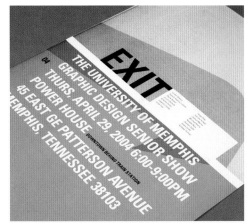

0801

0800

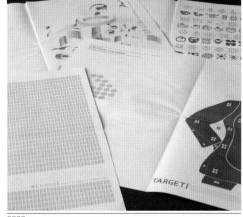

0802

0803	0804
Carter Wong Tomlin	Segura Inc.
UK	USA

0805	0806
Carter Wong Tomlin	Sagmeister Inc.
UK	USA

0803

0805

0804

0806

0807

Mehdi Saeedi
Iran

338/339

1000
Posters +
banners

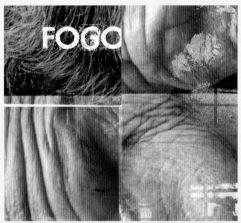

0808

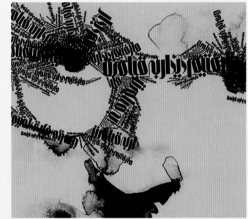

0810

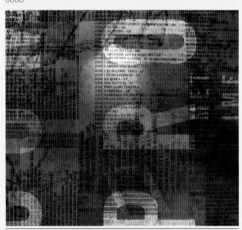

0809

0811

0812

Mike Salisbury, LLC
USA

340/341

1000
Posters +
banners

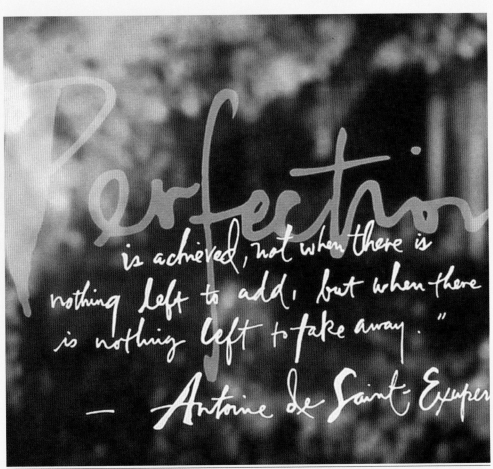

0813
Lippa Pearce Design, London
UK
↘

0814
Insight Design Communications
USA
↘↘

0815
Wonksite
Colombia
↘

0816
Segura Inc.
USA
↘↘

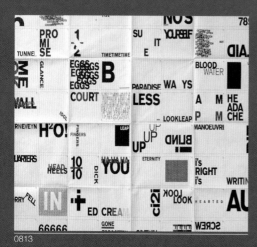

0813

0815

0814

0816

0817
Enspace, Inc.
USA
↘

0818
the commissary
USA
↘↘

0819
Scorsone/Drueding
USA
↘

0820
Frida Larios
El Salvador
↘↘

342/343
1000 Posters + banners

0817

0819

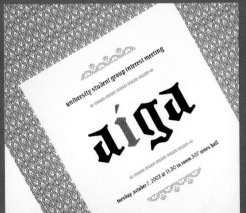

0818

0820

0821

0823

0822

0824

0825	0826	0827	0828	344/345
vo6	**Juan Torneros**	**WilsonHarvey/Loewy**	**WilsonHarvey/Loewy**	1000 Posters + banners
Brazil	Colombia	UK	UK	

↘ ↘↘ ↘ ↘↘

0825

0827

0826

0828

0829
the commissary
USA

0830
the commissary
USA

0831
the commissary
USA

0832
ALR Design
USA

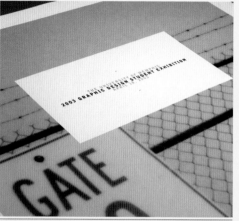

0829

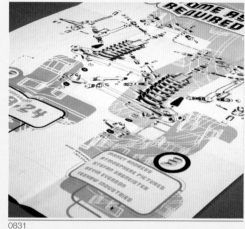

0831

0830

0832

0833
the commissary
USA

346/347

1000
Posters +
banners

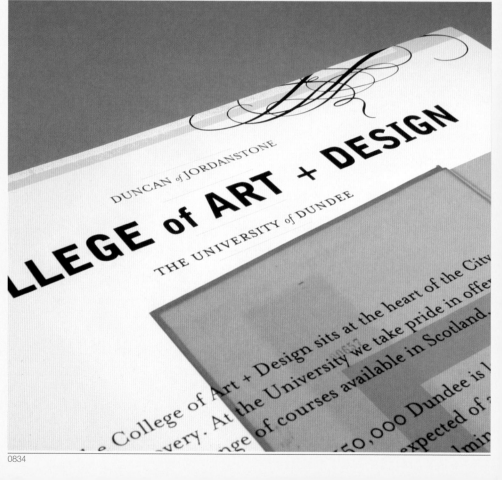

0835
the commissary
USA

348/349
1000
Posters +
banners

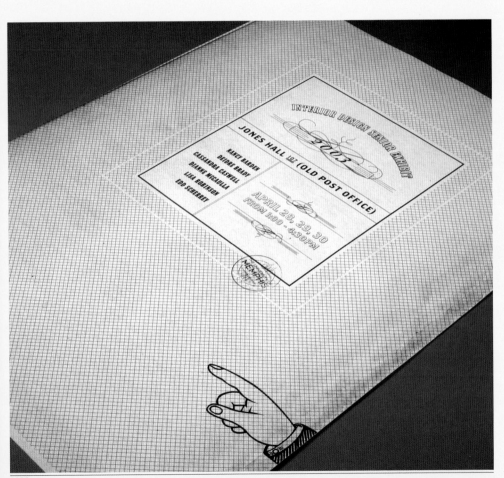

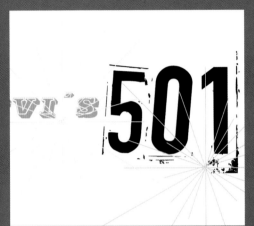

0837

0839

California Society of Printers — Ninetieth Annual — 1914–2004

0838

0840

0841
Dulude
Canada

0842
Iron Design
USA

0843
Capsule
USA

0844
Capsule
USA

0841

0843

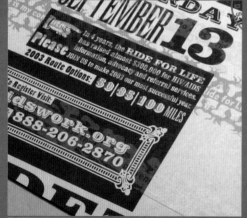

0842

0844

0845
Crush Design
UK
↘

0846
Wonksite
Colombia
↘↘

0847
Sagmeister Inc.
USA
↘

0848
Wonksite
Colombia
↘↘

352/353
1000
Posters +
banners

0845

0847

0846

0848

2004

SESSION 1, JUNE 7 - JULY 8

SESSION 2, JULY 13 - AUGUS'

SPECIALIZED STUDY COURSES FOR

MOTIONOGRAPHY

Instructor
LUCAS CHARLES

*Aesthetic and technical issues for effective
typographic communication in electronic media,
emphasis on relationship of form to content, special
consideration of time-based presentation and impact
of electronic interface.*

Days
MONDAY - FRIDAY

Time
10:45-2:00

REAL-WORLD-STUD

Instructor
GARY GOLIGHTLY

*Work under faculty supervision on projects f
institutional and corporate clients, assist in
developing publications, exhibits, signage and
other graphics, and participate in profession.
design process from project inception to comp*

Days
MONDAY - FRIDAY

Time
10:45-2:00

1000
Posters +
banners

MILTON THEATRE PRESENTS
MACBETH

DIRECTED BY COLIN GRAHAM
DESIGNER ARTHUR MACARTHUR
PRODUCER ALFRED LEEDING
LIGHTING BRIAN ARMSTRONG
CAST INCLUDES
DICK HAND
JUNE PEARCE
JANE WATERMAN

ESME MACARTHUR
STAN TURNER
NORMAN SLATER
KEN WILLIAMS
REG DUFF
BOB DAVIES
CHARLES SEARING
JO MILNER

9 SEPTEMBER–9 OCTOBER
BOX OFFICE
0145369 2380

0851
NB:Studio
UK

0852
AdamsMorioka, Inc.
USA

0853
Modern Dog
USA

0854
Joe Miller's Company
USA

0851

0853

0852

0854

0855

Segura Inc.
USA

356/357

1000
Posters +
banners

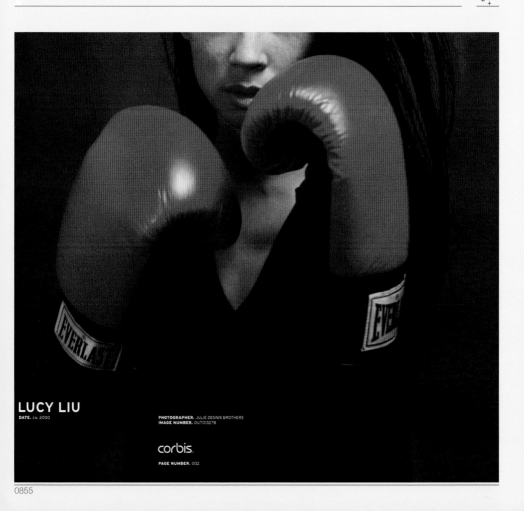

LUCY LIU
DATE. ca. 2000

PHOTOGRAPHER. JULIE DENNIS BROTHERS
IMAGE NUMBER. OUT013278

corbis.

PAGE NUMBER. 002

0857
Mehdi Saeedi
Iran

358/359
1000
Posters +
banners

Design Center Ltd.
Slovenia

↘

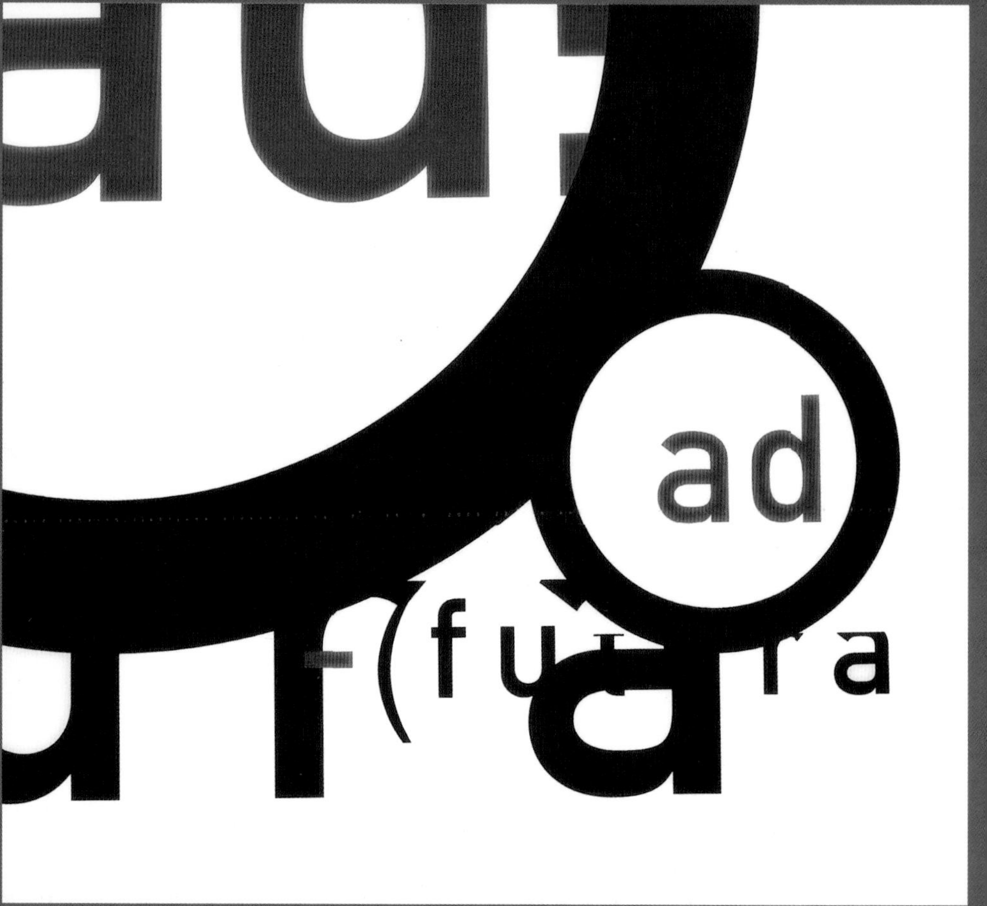

0859
KearneyRocholl Corporate Communications AG
Germany
↘

0860
KearneyRocholl Corporate Communications AG
Germany
↘↘

0861
KearneyRocholl Corporate Communications AG
Germany
↘

0862
KearneyRocholl Corporate Communications AG
Germany
↘↘

360/361
1000
Posters +
banners

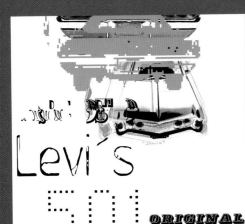

0859

0861

0860

0862

0864
Modern Dog
USA

↘

362/363

1000
Posters+
banners

0865

0867

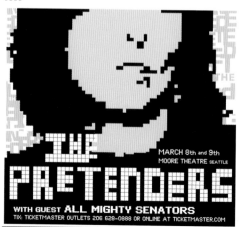

0866

0868

0869
vo6
Brazil

364/365

1:000
Posters+
banners

THE AMERICAN ACADEMY OF ARTS AND SCIENCES

THE GETTY CENTER FOR THE HISTORY OF ART AND THE HUMA

THE UNIVERSITY OF CALIFORNIA HUMANITIES RESEARCH INST

CENSORSHIP

SILENCING

PRACTICES OF CULTURAL REGULATION

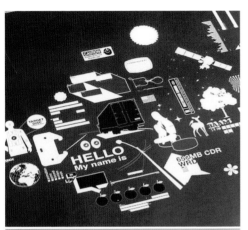

0871

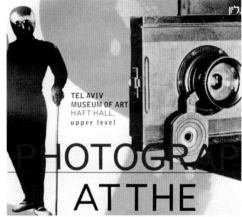

0873

0872

0874

0875

0877

0876

0878

0879
Chen Design Associates
USA

368/369
1000
Posters +
banners

0880
Joe Miller's Company
USA
↘

0881
344 Design, LLC
USA
↘↘

0882
Juan Torneros
Colombia
↘

0883
Segura Inc.
USA
↘↘

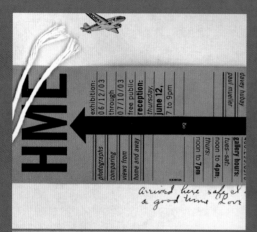

0880

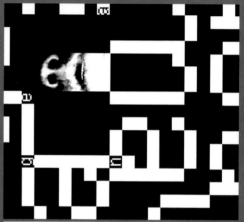

0882

0881

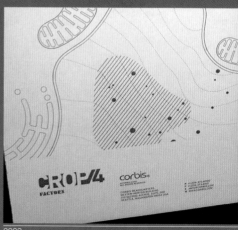

0883

0884
Segura Inc.
USA
↘

0885
**KearneyRocholl Corporate
Communications AG**
Germany
↘↘

0886
Segura Inc.
USA
↘

0887
**KearneyRocholl Corporate
Communications AG**
Germany
↘↘

370/371

1000
Posters +
banners

0884

0886

0885

0887

Chapter 6.
3D + outdoor + digital.

Packaging

Websites
>

Signage
>

Film

Television

Outdoor

Large format

3D

0888

0890

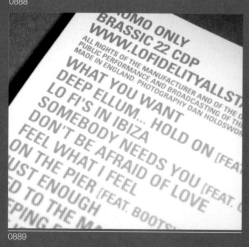

0889

0891

0892
Felton Communication
UK

0893
Lippa Pearce Design, London
UK

0894
Hoyne Design
Australia

0895
Machine
The Netherlands

374/375

100
outdoor +
digital

0892

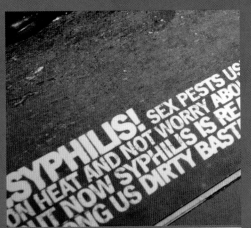

DYSFUNCTIONAL

K

TO REMOVE THE BIAS FROM THE UNIVERSE, PRESS DOWN
ON THE BLAME RELEASE BUTTON AND TURN THE CENTRE
OF GRAVITY CLOCKWISE. *The bias will slip off easily.*

WALKING WITH SHOES ON FIRE
CAN'T WAIT TO MEET YOU

SONG LYRIC 04

WALKING WITH SHOES ON FIRE
Walking with shoes on fire
Mercury rising higher
Every step is closer to you
I'm walking with shoes on fire

Has time stopped cold
The moments seem like lifetimes
I crave to hold you
No other thing fills my mind

Chorus
Walking with shoes on fire
Mercury rising higher
Every step is closer to you
I'm walking with shoes on fire

No ache, no cut
Has struck so deeply inside
To see, to touch you
No other piece will satisfy

I'm outside, lost in the dark night
An orphan who longs to come home
You draw me, capture and claim me
More than I've ever known

Chorus
Walking with shoes on fire
Mercury rising higher
Every step is closer to you
I'm walking with shoes on fire

0405

KEEP THIS BOOKLET HANDY FOR
REFERENCE UNTIL YOU HAVE MASTERED
THE ABILITY TO BE TOO DEMANDING.

0894

0893

KCUBE
1.FR33Z
2.ARP SURFACE

0895

0896
Felton Communication
UK

0897
Why Not Associates
UK

0898
Why Not Associates
UK

0899
Muggie Ramadani Design Studio
Denmark

0896

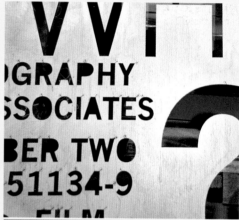

0898

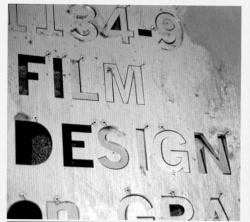

0897

0899

0900

0902

0901

0903

0905	0906	0907	0908	378/379
Harcus Design	**Sweden Graphics**	Sweden Graphics	**Harcus Design**	1:1000
Australia	Sweden	Sweden	Australia	3D +
				outdoor +
				digital

0905

0907

0906

0908

0909

0911

0910

0912

0913

Smith Design
USA

380/381

1000
3D +
outdoor +
digital

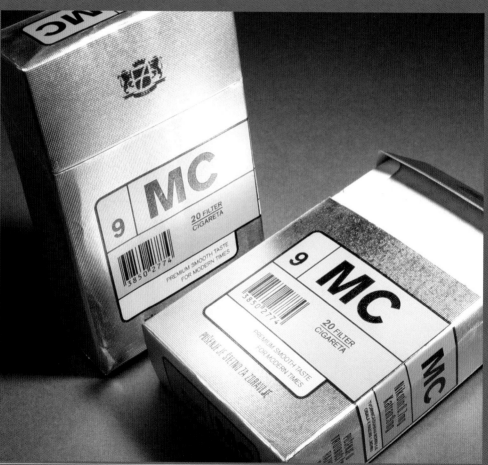

0915

0917

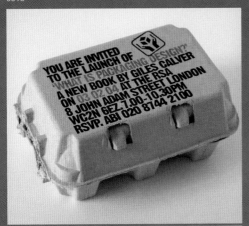

0916

0918

0919
unit 9
UK
↘

0920
**Hornall Anderson Design
Works, Inc.**
USA
↘

0921
Felton Communication
UK
↘

0922
**Hornall Anderson Design
Works, Inc.**
USA
↘

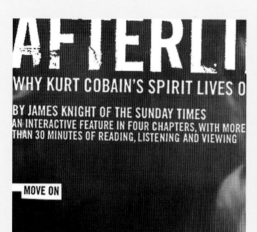

0919

0921

0920

0922

0923

0925

0924

0926

CLARO INTELECTO
PEDESTRIAN 2X12"

℗ 2004 Ai RECORDS. © 2004 Ai RECORDS. ALL WORK WRITTEN & PRODUCED BY MARK OF THE
STEWART. ALL RIGHTS OF THE ... RECORDED WORK RESERVED.
UNAUTHORISED COPYING ... OR RENTAL OF THIS RECORD-
ING PROHIBITED. DISTRIB... RDS PRODUCTS VISIT
HTTP://WWW.Ai...

PERCENTAGES
RESONATION
BAUDRILLARDS SUPPER
RIA
OTUX
SECTION
BACK
2. SECTION
3. YOU NOT ME
SECTION
NOBODY
YOUR TROPHY

0928

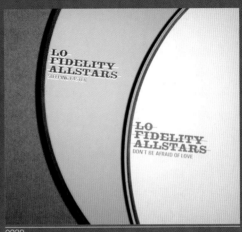

0930

0929

0931

0933
IAAH/iamalwayshungry
USA

↘

388/389
1000
3D +
outdoor +
digital

0934
Crush Design
UK

0935
WilsonHarvey/Loewy
UK

0936
Crush Design
UK

0937
Plan-B Studio
UK

0934

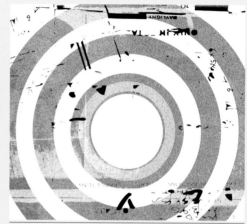

0936

0935

0937

0938
WilsonHarvey/Loewy
UK

390/391

1000
3D+
outdoor +
digital

0939
**Muggie Ramadani
Design Studio**
Denmark
↘

0940
Marius Fahrner Design
Germany
↘↘

0941
Capsule
USA
↘

0942
Crush Design
UK
↘↘

0939

0941

0940

0942

0943

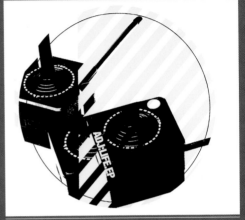

0945

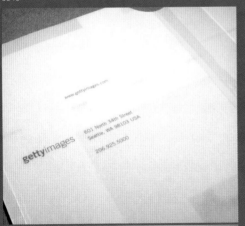

0944

0946

0947
Carter Wong Tomlin
UK

0948
Jason Smith
UK

0949
**Lippa Pearce
Design, London**
UK

0950
Ai Records
UK

0947

0949

0948

0950

0951
Ai Records
UK
↘

0952
Why Not Associates
UK
↘↘

0953
Ai Records
UK
↘

0954
Why Not Associates
UK
↘↘

394/395

1000
outdoor +
digital

0951

FZV:PRECEDENT.
(P) 2004 Ai RECORDS. © 2004 Ai RECORDS. ALPOOL 44KHZ. WRITTEN & PRODUCED BY RICHARD HERBERT. ALL RIGHTS OF THE PRODUCER AND OF THE OWNER OF THE RECORDED WORK RESERVED. UNAUTHORISED COPYING, PUBLIC PERFORMANCE, BROADCASTING, HIRING OR RENTAL OF THIS RECORDING PROHIBITED. DISTRIBUTED BY BAKED GOODS. FOR MORE INFO BUY Ai.RECORDS PRODUCTS VISIT WWW.AIRECORDS.COM / WWW.ANATHEMATICA.COM

Ai

1. METAPHRASTIC.
2. ISO R2.
3. COL MODULUS.
4. AMLGM2.
5. WLTMLT VERSION.
6. COLD.
7. COLDER STILL.
8. CLATR2.
9. SELLS BORROWS.
10. GOLD TO RUST.
11. F2V.
12. UNTITLED [11.01.01].
13. SHE SAID2.
14. F2V-8BIT.

0953

0952

0954

0957
Juicy Temples Creative
USA

0958
Juicy Temples Creative
USA

0959
Juicy Temples Creative
USA

0960
Juicy Temples Creative
USA

HEATHER
GOLDEN
A TESTAMENT OF
STRENGTH
+FLEXIBILITY

★ NEW BIZ

STAYS COOL
WHEN THE HEAT'S
TURNED UP
SMOOTH SAILING

CELEBRATE
A GOOD DAY

0957

ANTHONY
DeLAURA
RESIDENT FLASH GURU
ALL AROUND
NICE GUY
DESIGNER

CREATIVE ABILIT
COMPLIMENT
TECHNICAL
WIZARDRY

★ YES, IT'S DANGEROUS,

0959

WHEN
RANDY
J. HUNT

STROLLS INTO THE STUDIO,
HE BRINGS WITH HIM A COOL CHARM
+YOUTHFUL EXUBERANCE
HIS ENERGY IS CONTAGIOUS
HIS ENTHUSIASM IS INFECTIOUS
AND HE'S A DAMN FINE
DESIGNER
TOO.

★ NOT ANGRY

0958

SIT UP AND
TAKE NOTICE.
KLAUS HEESCH
TWO-FISTED ROGUE
OWNER / ART DIRECTOR
★HONEST★
TRUE
PROBLEM
SOLVER
DESIGN
EXPERTISE
CREATIVE WISDOM

MOTORCYCLIST
MUSICIAN
DOG★OWNER

0960

0961

WilsonHarvey/Loewy
UK

398/399
1000
3D +
outdoor +
digital

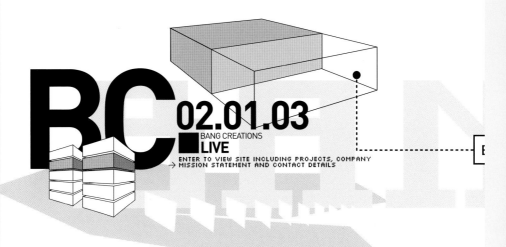

0963
WilsonHarvey/Loewy
UK

400/401

1000
3D+
outdoor +
digital

0965	0966	0967	0968	402/403

0965
Hoyne Design
Australia

0966
Sweden Graphics
Sweden

0967
Marino A. Gallo
USA

0968
Hoyne Design
Australia

1000
1D +
outdoor +
digital

0965

0967

0966

0968

0969	0970
Ai Records	**Lippa Pearce Design, London**
UK	UK

0971	0972
Crush Design	**The Family Design International**
UK	UK

0969

0971

0970

0972

0973

Non-Format
UK

404/405

1000
3D+
outdoor+
digital

01. Saw Song 02. I Blame You Not 03. Alive 04. Bonding
05. It's Time 06. Lost To Sea 07. June 15 08. Bravely Born(e)
09. Pianni 10. Baby Bloodheart 11. For Me

AC12CD ℗ 2004 Accidental © 2004 Accidental Barcode: 827884001028 Made in EU
www.magicandaccident.com www.maracarlyle.com

accidental

0975
Ai Records
UK

406/407
1000
3D +
outdoor +
digital

CLARO.
INTELECTO.
A1. CHICAGO
A2. SECTION [PART 2]
B1. MONO
B2. SENTI

0976

0978

0977

0979

0980

The Kitchen
UK

408/409

1000
3D+
outdoor
+
digital

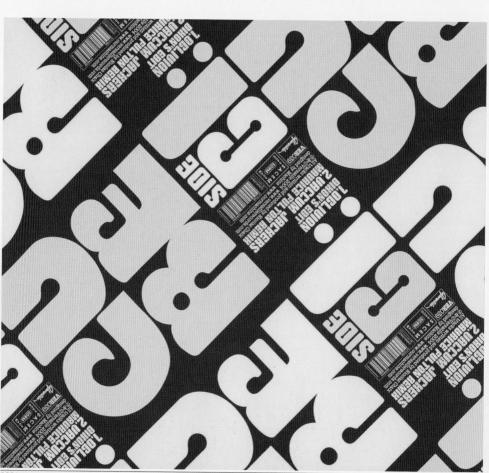

0982

Hoyne Design
Australia

410/411

1000
3D +
outdoor +
digital

0983
Wonksite
Colombia

0984
Wonksite
Colombia

0985
Wonksite
Colombia

0986
Wonksite
Colombia

0983

0985

0984

0986

0987
Wonksite
Colombia

0988
Wonksite
Colombia

0989
Dulude
Canada

0990
Dulude
Canada

412/413
1000
3D +
outdoor +
digital

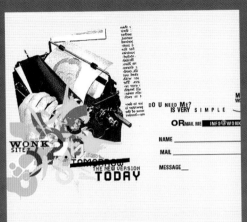

0987

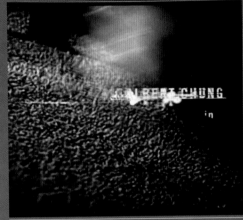

0989

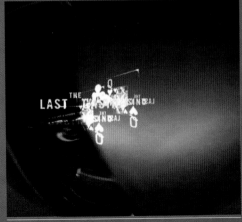

0988

0990

0991
Dulude
Canada

0992
Dulude
Canada

0993
Dulude
Canada

0994
Dulude
Canada

0991

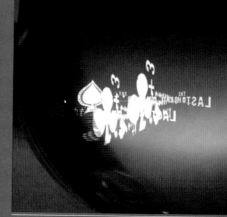

0992

0994

0995
Why Not
Associates
UK
↘

0996
Why Not
Associates
UK
↘↘

0997
Why Not
Associates
UK
↘

0998
Wonksite
Colombia
↘↘

414/415

1000
3D +
outdoor +
digital

0995

0997

0996

0998

|01|02|03|
NEWS

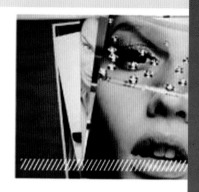

WIE KAMEN SIE ZUM DESIGN?

Ich hatte mit 20 eine Ausgabe der ital[ien]schen Vogue in der Hand, doppelt so [dick] wie die deutsche Ausgabe und voller i[nte]ressanter Bilder. Das hat einen verbor[ge]nen Code in mir aktiviert und mir war sofort klar, ich wollte auch so etwas machen: Images kreieren.

INTRO	01	02	03	04

1000
KearneyRocholl Corporate Communications AG
Germany

416/417
1000
3D+
outdoor
+

Index.

Designers
Alan and Amanda Altman
Client
Jodi Henning
Tools/Software/Platform
Adobe Photoshop, Adobe Illustrator
Fonts
Trade Gothic, Mrs. Eaves, Univers

0095
Art Director
Alan Altman
Designers
Alan and Amanda Altman
Client
A3 Design
Tools/Software/Platform
Adobe Photoshop, Adobe Illustrator
Fonts
Trade Gothic, Tanek

0775
Art Director
Alan Altman
Designer
Alan Altman
Client
Amanda Altman
Tools/Software/Platform
Adobe Photoshop, Adobe Illustrator
Fonts
Trade Gothic, Tanek, Franklin Gothic

0781
Art Director
Alan Altman
Designer
Alan Altman
Client
Amanda Altman
Tools/Software/Platform
Adobe Photoshop, Adobe Illustrator
Font
Trade Gothic, Tanek, Franklin Gothic

Aboud Sodano
0230
Art Director
Alan Aboud
Designers
Ellie Ridsdale
Alan Aboud
Client
Paul Smith

Academy of Art University
0414
Instructor
Todd Hedgpeth
Designer
Amy Lee
Client
Student Work
Tools/Software/Platform
Adobe InDesign, Adobe Photoshop, Adobe Illustrator
Font
Adobe Garamond

0432
Instructor
Kathryn Morgan
Designer
Amy Lee
Client
Student Work
Tools/Software/Platform
Adobe InDesign, Adobe Illustrator, Adobe Photoshop
Font
Centaur

0918
Instructor
Todd Hedgpeth
Designer
Amy Lee
Client
Student Work
Tools/Software/Platform
Adobe InDesign, Adobe Photoshop, Adobe Illustrator
Font
Adobe Garamond

0956
Instructor
Thomas McNutty
Designer
Amy Lee
Client
Student Work
Tools/Software/Platform
Adobe Illustrator
Font
Calligraphy

AdamsMorioka, Inc.
0322
Art Directors
Sean Adams, Noreen Morioka
Designer
Sean Adams
Client
Southern California Institute of Architecture
Tools/Software/Platform
Adobe Pagemaker
Font
Trade Gothic Condensed

0420
Art Director
Noreen Morioka
Designers
Noreen Morioka, Volker Durre
Client
Fred Seibert
Tools/Software/Platform
Adobe Illustrator
Fonts
Poplar, Blackoak, Birch, Cottonwood

0647
Art Director
Sean Adams
Designer
Sean Adams
Client
Mohawk Paper
Tools/Software/Platform
Adobe Pagemaker
Fonts
Monotype, Baskerville, Young Baroque

0735
Art Directors
Sean Adams, Noreen Morioka
Designers
Sean Adams, Volker Durre
Client
Nickelodeon
Tools/Software/Platform
Adobe Illustrator, Adobe Pagemaker
Fonts
Trade Gothic, Clarendon, Folio, News Gothic

0852
Art Directors
Sean Adams, Noreen Morioka
Designers
Sean Adams, Volker Durre
Client
Slamdance Film Festival
Tools/Software/Platform
Adobe Illustrator, Adobe Pagemaker
Font
Monotype Grotesque

0870
Art Directors
Sean Adams, Noreen Morioka
Designer
Sean Adams
Client
The Getty
Tools/Software/Platform
Adobe Illustrator
Font
Trade Gothic

Ai Records
0927
Art Director
Jason Smith
Designer
Jason Smith
Client
Ai Records
Tools/Software/Platform
QuarkXPress, Adobe Photoshop
Font
Helvetica Neue

0943
Art Director
Jason Smith
Designer
Jason Smith
Client
Ai Records
Tools/Software/Platform
Adobe Illustrator
Font
Helvetica Neue

0945
Art Director
Jason Smith
Designer
Jason Smith
Client
Ai Records
Tools/Software/Platform
QuarkXPress, Adobe Photoshop
Font
Helvetica Neue

0946
Art Director
Jason Smith
Designer
Jason Smith
Client
Ai Records
Tools/Software/Platform
Adobe Illustrator Flash
Font
Akzidenz

0950
Art Director
Jason Smith
Designer
Jason Smith
Client
Ai Records
Tools/Software/Platform
QuarkXPress, Adobe Photoshop
Font
Helvetica Neue

0951
Art Director
Jason Smith
Designer
Jason Smith
Client
Ai Records
Tools/Software/Platform
Adobe Illustrator
Font
Helvetica Neue

0953
Art Director
Jason Smith
Designer
Jason Smith
Client
Ai Records
Tools/Software/Platform
QuarkXPress, Adobe Illustrator
Font
Akzidenz

0969
Art Director
Jason Smith
Designer
Jason Smith
Client
Ai Records
Tools/Software/Platform
QuarkXPress, Adobe Illustrator
Font
Helvetica Neue

0975
Art Director
Jason Smith
Designer
Jason Smith
Client
Ai Records
Tools/Software/Platform
Adobe Illustrator

Aloof Designs
0257
Art Director
Sam Aloof
Designers
Robin Ek, Joakim Sjogren
Client
Georgina Goodman
Paper/Materials
Colorplan 2EN Text, Greyboard Cover, End Pages

0316
Art Director
Sam Aloof
Designers
Robin Ek, Joakim Sjogren
Client
Georgina Goodman
Paper/Materials
Colorplan 2EN Text, Greyboard Cover, End Pages
Font
Akzidenz Grotesk

ALR Design
0002
Art Director
Noah Scalin
Designer
Noah Scalin
Client
Katherine Profeta
Tools/Software/Platform
Adobe Photoshop
Font
Rosewood (combined with elements of Shelley Volante Script)

0006
Art Director
Noah Scalin
Designer
Noah Scalin
Client
Katherine Profeta
Tools/Software/Platform
Adobe Photoshop
Font
Rosewood (combined with elements of Shelley Volante Script)

0007
Art Director
Noah Scalin
Designer
Noah Scalin
Client
Salt Theater
Tools/Software/Platform
Adobe Photoshop, QuarkXPress
Font
based on Razorsuite

0074
Art Director
Noah Scalin
Designer
Noah Scalin
Client
Artspace
Tools/Software/Platform
QuarkXPress, Adobe Photoshop/Mac
Fonts
Hand re-drawn Univers, Signpainter, Akzidenz Grotesk, Futura + Univers and Inside Out

0168
Art Director
Noah Scalin
Designer
Noah Scalin
Client
Salt Theater
Tools/Software/Platform
Adobe Photoshop, QuarkXPress/Mac
Font
based on Razorsuite

0185
Art Director
Noah Scalin
Designer
Noah Scalin
Client
Legend Entertainment
Tools/Software/Platform
Adobe Illustrator/Mac
Font
Akzidenz Grotesk

0832
Art Director
Noah Scalin
Designer
Noah Scalin
Client
New Georges
Tools/Software/Platform
Adobe Photoshop
Fonts
Univers, Presstype Helvetica

And Partners
0147
Art Director
David Schimmel
Designer
David Schimmel
Client
Vincent Ricardel
Tools/Software/Platform
QuarkXPress/Mac G4
Fonts
Garamond, Trade Gothic

0152
Art Director
David Schimmel
Designer
David Schimmel
Client
Driven Industries Inc.
Tools/Software/Platform
Adobe Illustrator, Quark/Mac G4
Font
Futura

0153
Art Director
David Schimmel
Designer
Chariss Gibiliso
Client
Wall Street Rising
Tools/Software/Platform
Adobe Illustrator/Mac G4
Font
Din (family)

0425
Art Director
David Schimmel
Designer
David Schimmel
Client
DAS Graphics
Tools/Software/Platform
Freehand
Font
Univers

0688
Art Director
David Schimmel
Designers
Chariss Gibilisco, Susan Brzozowski
Client
National Council of Jewish Women
Tools/Software/Platform
QuarkXPress, Adobe Photoshop
Font
Gills Sans, Trad Gothic

0691
Art Director
David Schimmel
Designers
Chariss Gibilisco, Susan Brzozowski
Client
National Council of Jewish Women
Tools/Software/Platform
QuarkXPress, Adobe Photoshop
Font
Gills Sans, Trad Gothic

0706
Art Director
David Schimmel
Designer
David Schimmel
Client
And Partners
Tools/Software/Platform
QuarkXPress
Font
Univers

0738
Art Director
David Schimmel
Designer
Chariss Gibilisco
Client
American Committee for the Weizmann Institute of Science
Tools/Software/Platform
Adobe Illustrator
Fonts
Weiss, Gill Sans

Anna B. Design
0501
Art Director
Anna Berkenbusch
Designers
Anna Berkenbusch, Tina Wende
Client
Maikaferflieg E.V.
Tools/Software/Platform
QuarkXPress
Fonts
Officina Sans, Compacta

0502
Art Director
Anna Berkenbusch
Designers
Anna Berkenbusch, Tina Wende
Client
Maikaferflieg E.V.
Tools/Software/Platform
QuarkXPress
Fonts
Officina Sans, Compacta

0605
Art Director
Anna Berkenbusch
Designers
Anna Berkenbusch, Tina Wende
Client
Maikaferflieg E.V.
Tools/Software/Platform
QuarkXPress
Fonts
Officina Sans, Compacta

Atelier Works
0890
Art Director
Ian Chilvers
Designer
Joseph Luffman
Client
Slade Gardens
Tools/Software/Platform
QuarkXPress
Font
Champion

Aufuldish & Warriner

0085
Designer
Bob Aufuldish
Client
California College of the Arts and Crafts
Tools/Software/Platform
Adobe Illustrator, Adobe Photoshop/Mac OS
Paper/Materials
Titan Dull White Book

0101
Art Director
Bob Aufuldish
Designer
Bob Aufuldish
Client
California College of the Arts and Crafts
Tools/Software/Platform
Adobe Illustrator, Adobe Photoshop/Mac OS
Fonts
New Century Schoolbook, Interstate

0141
Art Director
Bob Aufuldish
Designer
Bob Aufuldish
Client
California College of the Arts and Crafts
Tools/Software/Platform
Adobe Illustrator, Adobe Photoshop/Mac OS
Fonts
VAG Rounded, Vendetta, Clarendon

0741
Art Director
Bob Aufuldish
Designer
Bob Aufuldish
Client
University of Denver Victoria H. Myhren Gallery
Tools/Software/Platform
Adobe InDesign
Fonts
Bulmer, Latin MT, Clarendon, Bodoni Poster, Bodoni Egyptian Shadow, Gothic Round, Champion

0742
Art Director
Bob Aufuldish
Designer
Bob Aufuldish
Client
University of Denver Victoria H. Myhren Gallery
Tools/Software/Platform
Adobe InDesign
Fonts
Bulmer, Latin MT, Clarendon, Bodoni Poster, Bodoni Egyptian Shadow, Gothic Round, Champion

BBK Studio
0662
Art Directors
Yang Kim
Designers
Yang Kim
Client
Jack Ridl
Tools/Software/Platform
QuarkXPress/Mac
Font
Humanist

0667
Art Directors
Steve Frykholm, Yang Kim
Designers
Yang Kim, Michele Chartier
Client
Herman Miller
Tools/Software/Platform
QuarkXPress, Adobe Photoshop
Font
Avenir

Be Design
0396
Art Director
Eric Read
Designer
Deborah Smith Read
Client
Karma Creaions
Tools/Software/Platform
Adobe Illustrator
Font
Customized

Beautiful
0748
Art Director
Kerry Roper
Designer
Kerry Roper
Client
Pinko
Tools/Software/Platform
Adobe Photoshop, Adobe Illustrator
Font
Tsjecho

0751
Art Director
Kerry Roper
Designer
Kerry Roper
Client
Net Magazine
Tools/Software/Platform
Adobe Photoshop, Adobe Illustrator
Font
Hand drawn

0752
Art Director
Kerry Roper
Designer
Kerry Roper
Client
The Big Issue
Tools/Software/Platform
Adobe Photoshop, Adobe Illustrator
Font
Hand Drawn

0753
Art Director
Kerry Roper
Designer
Kerry Roper
Client
Onboard Magazine
Tools/Software/Platform
Adobe Photoshop, Adobe Illustrator
Font
Gold Rush, Mesquite

0754
Art Director
Kerry Roper
Designer
Kerry Roper
Client
Universal Records/Mercury Records
Tools/Software/Platform
Adobe Photoshop, Adobe Illustrator
Font
Mesquite

0755
Art Director
Kerry Roper
Designer
Kerry Roper
Client
Beautiful
Tools/Software/Platform
Adobe Photoshop, Adobe Illustrator
Font
Avenir

0753
Art Director
Kerry Roper
Designer
Kerry Roper
Client
The Big Issue
Tools/Software/Platform
Adobe Photoshop, Adobe Illustrator
Font
Hand Drawn (in chocolate)

0757
Art Director
Kerry Roper
Designer
Kerry Roper
Client
Bulgaria Magazine
Tools/Software/Platform
Adobe Photoshop, Adobe Illustrator
Fonts
Tempo Mono, hand drawn

Belyea
0977
Art Director
Patricia Belyea
Designer
Naomi Murphy
Client
Imperial Lithograph
Tools/Software/Platform
Adobe Illustrator
Paper/Materials
Westvaco, Sterling Ultra, Dull 100C for wrap and calendar pages
Font
Hand drawn

Bisqit Design
0040
Art Director
Daphne Diamant
Designer
Michael Morgan
Client
Bisqit Design
Tools/Software/Platform
QuarkXPress
Font
Helvetica Neue LT 55 Roman/95 Black

Blackletter

Design Inc.
0237
Art Directors
Ken Bessie, Rick Sealock
Designer
Ken Bessie
Client
Rick Sealock Piglet Press
Tools/Software/Platform
QuarkXPress, Adobe Illustrator, Adobe Photoshop

0269
Art Directors
Ken Bessie, Rick Sealock
Designer
Ken Bessie
Client
Rick Sealock Piglet Press
Tools/Software/Platform
QuarkXPress, Adobe Illustrator, Adobe Photoshop

0270
Art Directors
Ken Bessie, Rick Sealock
Designer
Ken Bessie
Client
Rick Sealock Piglet Press
Tools/Software/Platform
QuarkXPress, Adobe Illustrator, Adobe Photoshop

0271
Art Directors
Ken Bessie, Rick Sealock
Designer
Ken Bessie
Client
Rick Sealock Piglet Press
Tools/Software/Platform
QuarkXPress, Adobe Illustrator, Adobe Photoshop

0272
Art Directors
Ken Bessie, Rick Sealock
Designer
Ken Bessie
Client
Rick Sealock Piglet Press
Tools/Software/Platform
QuarkXPress, Adobe Illustrator, Adobe Photoshop

0273
Art Directors
Ken Bessie, Rick Sealock
Designer
Ken Bessie
Client
Rick Sealock Piglet Press
Tools/Software/Platform
QuarkXPress, Adobe Illustrator, Adobe Photoshop

0274
Art Directors
Ken Bessie, Rick Sealock
Designer
Ken Bessie
Client
Rick Sealock Piglet Press
Tools/Software/Platform
QuarkXPress, Adobe Illustrator, Adobe Photoshop

0275
Art Directors
Ken Bessie, Rick Sealock
Designer
Ken Bessie
Client
Rick Sealock Piglet Press
Tools/Software/Platform
QuarkXPress, Adobe Illustrator, Adobe Photoshop

Blok Design
0022
Art Director
Vanessa Eckstein
Designer
Vanessa Eckstein
Client
The Nienkatver Store

0050
Art Director
Vanessa Eckstein
Designers
Vanessa Eckstein, Frances Chen
Client
RGD/Ontario
Tools/Software/Platform
Adobe Illustrator
Paper/Materials
Cougar

0052
Art Director
Vanessa Eckstein
Designers
Vanessa Eckstein, Frances Chen
Client
RGD/Ontario
Tools/Software/Platform
Adobe Illustrator
Paper/Materials
Cougar

0060
Art Director
Vanessa Eckstein
Designers
Vanessa Eckstein, Frances Chen
Client
RGD/Ontario
Tools/Software/Platform
Adobe Illustrator
Paper/Materials
Cougar

0418
Art Director
Vanessa Eckstein
Designers
Vanessa Eckstein
Client
Distrito Films

0403
Art Director
Vanessa Eckstein
Designers
Vanessa Eckstein, Frances Chen, Stephanie Young
Client
Ni're Mexico

The Production Kitchen
Tools/Software/Platform
Adobe Illustrator
Paper/Materials
Beckett Expression

0445
Art Director
Vanessa Eckstein
Designers
Vanessa Eckstein, Mariana Congegni
Client
Centro

0471
Art Director
Vanessa Eckstein
Designer
Vanessa Eckstein
Client
Distrito Films

0474
Art Director
Vanessa Eckstein
Designers
Vanessa Eckstein, Frances Chen
Client
El Zanson
Tools/Software/Platform
Adobe Illustrator
Paper/Materials
Strathmore Ultimate White

0479
Art Director
Vanessa Eckstein
Designers
Vanessa Eckstein, Mariana Congegni
Client
Centro

0482
Art Director
Vanessa Eckstein
Designers
Vanessa Eckstein, Frances Chen, Stephanie Young
Client
Blok Design
Tools/Software/Platform
Adobe Illustrator

0528
Art Director
Vanessa Eckstein
Designers
Vanessa Eckstein, Mariana Congegni
Client
Ni're Mexico

0529
Art Director
Vanessa Eckstein
Designers
Vanessa Eckstein
Client
Ni're Mexico

0530
Art Director
Vanessa Eckstein
Designers
Vanessa Eckstein, Mariana Congegni
Client
Ni're Mexico

0531
Art Director
Vanessa Eckstein
Designers
Vanessa Eckstein, Mariana Congegni
Client
Ni're Mexico

0798
Art Directors
Vanessa Eckstein
Designers
Vanessa Eckstein, Mariana Congegni
Client
Centro

Blue River
0496
Art Director
James Askham
Designer
James Askham
Client
Baltic Centre for Contemporary Art
Tools/Software/Platform
QuarkXPress
Fonts
Akzidenz Grotesk, Baltic Affisch

0607
Art Director
James Askham
Designer
James Askham
Client
Baltic Centre for Contemporary Art
Tools/Software/Platform
QuarkXPress
Fonts
Akzidenz Grotesk, Baltic Affisch

Bright Pink
0069
Art Director
Jessica Glaser
Designers
Jessica Glaser, Carolyn Knight
Client
Bright Pink
Tools/Software/Platform
Adobe Illustrator

Bruketa & Zini
0226
Art Directors
Davor Buketa, Nikola Zini
Designer
Davor Buketa, Nikola Zini
Client
Podravka dd.
Tools/Software/Platform
Freehand, Adobe Photoshop
Paper/Materials
Agripina

0599
Art Directors
Davor Buketa, Nikola Zini
Designer
Davor Buketa, Nikola Zini
Client
Podravka dd.
Tools/Software/Platform
Freehand, QuarkXPress
Font
Tribeca

0601
Art Directors

Christine Fent, Manja Uellpap, Gilmar Wendt
Client
ISTD
Tools/Software/Platform
QuarkXPress/Mac
Fonts
Architype
Tschichold,
Augustea

Circle K Studio

0059
Art Director
Julie Keenan
Designer
Julie Keenan
Client
Circle K Studio
Tools/Software/Platform
Adobe Illustrator
Paper/Materials
Rubber Stamp Sewn

0102
Art Director
Julie Keenan
Designer
Julie Keenan
Client
Jamie Schulman,
Deborah Dalfen
Tools/Software/Platform
Adobe Illustrator
Paper/Materials
Custom Rubber
Stamp

0683
Art Director
Julie Keenan
Designer
Julie Keenan
Client
The University of
Maryland School of
Pharmacy
Tools/Software/Platform
QuarkXPress

Concrete (Chicago)

0077
Art Director
Jilly Simons
Designers
Jilly Simons, Regan
Todd
Client
Concrete
Tools/Software/Platform
QuarkXPress 4.1/
Mac OS 9.2
Fonts
Dalliance Script,
Franklin Gothic

0084
Art Director
Jilly Simons
Designers
Jilly Simons, Regan
Todd
Client
School of
Architecture,
Washington
University in St. Louis
Tools/Software/Platform
QuarkXPress
Fonts
Univers (BQ), Quay
Sans

0419
Art Director
Jilly Simons

Designers
Jilly Simons, Regan
Todd
Client
MSP Paris, SAS
Tools/Software/Platform
QuarkXPress, Adobe
Illustrator
Fonts
Univers, hand drawn
(logo)

0635
Art Director
Jilly Simons
Designers
Jilly Simons, Regan
Todd
Client
Hinge
Tools/Software/Platform
QuarkXPress
Fonts
Cochin Grotesque
MT Condensed,
Futura, Avenir, Letter
Gothic, Univers
Condensed

0636
Art Director
Jilly Simons
Designers
Jilly Simons, Regan
Todd
Client0140
Hinge
Tools/Software/Platform
QuarkXPress
Fonts
Cochin Grotesque
MT Condensed,
Futura, Avenir, Letter
Gothic, Univers
Condensed

Crush Design

0145
Art Director
Chris Pelling
Designer
Chris Pelling
Client
CamronPR
Tools/Software/Platform
Adobe Photoshop,
Adobe Illustrator,
QuarkXPress

0331
Art Director
Carl Rush
Designer
Carl Rush
Client
Harvill Publishing
Tools/Software/Platform
Adobe Illustrator,
Adobe Photoshop
Paper/Materials
Matt Laminate,
emboss

0453
Art Director
Carl Rush
Designer
Carl Rush
Client
Wea Records
Tools/Software/Platform
Adobe Illustrator

0454
Art Director
Carl Rush
Designer
Chris Pelling
Client
William Grant & Sons

Tools/Software/Platform
Adobe Illustrator

0455
Art Director
Carl Rush
Designer
Carl Rush
Client
Palm Pictures
Tools/Software/Platform
Adobe Photoshop
Paper/Materials
Paper, scissors

0456
Art Director
Carl Rush
Designer
Carl Rush
Client
Palm Pictures
Tools/Software/Platform
Adobe Illustrator

0457
Art Director
Carl Rush
Designer
Simon Scater
Client
William Grant & Sons
Tools/Software/Platform
Adobe Illustrator

0458
Art Director
Carl Rush
Designer
Simon Scater
Client
Heineken
International
Tools/Software/Platform
Adobe Illustrator

0459
Art Director
Carl Rush
Designer
Simon Scater
Client
William Grant & Sons
Tools/Software/Platform
Adobe Illustrator

0460
Art Director
Carl Rush
Designer
Tim Diacon
Client
Heineken
International
Tools/Software/Platform
Adobe Illustrator

0486
Art Director
Carl Rush
Designer
Tim Diacon
Client
Splendid
Communications
Tools/Software/Platform
Adobe Illustrator

0845
Art Director
Carl Rush
Designer
Carl Rush
Client
Self Promotion
Tools/Software/Platform
Adobe Photoshop

0865
Art Director

Carl Rush
Designer
Tim Diacon
Client
The Music Matrix
Tools/Software/Platform
Adobe Photoshop

0868
Art Director
Carl Rush
Designer
Tim Diacon
Client
The Music Matrix
Tools/Software/Platform
Adobe Photoshop

0909
Art Director
Carl Rush
Designer
Simon Scater
Client
Playlab/Toy2r
Paper/Materials
Spray Paint, Letraset

0934
Art Director
Carl Rush
Designer
Chris Pelling
Client
Full on Films
Tools/Software/Platform
Adobe Illustrator,
Adobe Photoshop,
Adobe After Effects

0936
Art Director
Carl Rush
Designer
Carl Rush
Client
Palm Pictures
Tools/Software/Platform
Adobe Photoshop
Paper/Materials
Photocopier

0942
Art Director
Carl Rush
Designer
Carl Rush
Client
Palm Pictures
Tools/Software/Platform
Adobe Photoshop

0971
Art Director
Carl Rush
Designer
Chris Pelling
Client
Full on Films
Tools/Software/Platform
Adobe Illustrator,
Adobe Photoshop,
Adobe After Effects

Danielle Foushee Design

0371
Art Director
Danielle Foushee
Designer
Danielle Foushee
Client
Danielle Foushee
Tools/Software/Platform
Adobe Illustrator,
Adobe InDesign

Carl Rush
Designer
Tim Diacon
Client
The Music Matrix
Tools/Software/Platform
Adobe Photoshop

David Salafia/ Laura Salafia

0051
Art Director
David Salafia, Laura
Salafia
Designer
David Salafia, Laura
Salafia
Client
David Salafia, Laura
Salafia
Tools/Software/Platform
Quark 4/Mac
Fonts
Mantinia, Mrs. Eaves

Design Center

0769
Art Director
Eduard Cehovin
Designer
Eduard Cehovin
Client
One Man-Show on
Billboard
Tools/Software/Platform
Adobe Illustrator

0858
Art Director
Eduard Cehovin
Designer
Eduard Cehovin
Client
One Man-Show on
Billboard
Tools/Software/Platform
Adobe Illustrator

0874
Art Director
Eduard Cehovin
Designer
Eduard Cehovin
Client
One Man-Show on
Billboard
Tools/Software/Platform
Adobe Illustrator

Design Depot Creative Bureau

0627
Art Director
Petr Bankov
Designer
Petr Bankov
Client
Design Depot

0628
Art Director
Petr Bankov
Designer
Petr Bankov
Client
Design Depot

0629
Art Director
Petr Bankov
Designer
Petr Bankov
Client
Design Depot

Design hoch- drei GmbH & Co.KG

0739
Art Directors
Wolfram Schaeffer,
Marcus Wichmann

Designer
Marcus Wichmann
Client
Daimler Chrysler AG
Tools/Software/Platform
QuarkXPress,
Feehand, Adobe
Photoshop
Font
Corporate S

Dynamo

0073
Art Director
Brian Nolan
Designer
Brian Nolan
Client
Amanda Brady
Tools/Software/Platform
Quark
Font
Garamond

D-Fuse

0035
Art Director
Mike Faulkner
Designer
Mike Faulkner
Client
D-Fuse
Tools/Software/Platform
Adobe Photoshop,
Freehand
Font
Franklin

0043
Art Director
Mike Faulkner
Designer
Mike Faulkner
Client
D-Fuse
Tools/Software/Platform
Adobe Photoshop,
Freehand
Font
Franklin

0044
Art Director
Mike Faulkner
Designer
Mike Faulkner
Client
D-Fuse
Tools/Software/Platform
Adobe Photoshop,
Freehand
Font
Franklin

0090
Art Director
Mike Faulkner
Designer
Mike Faulkner
Client
D-Fuse
Tools/Software/Platform
Adobe Photoshop,
Freehand
Font
Franklin

Dovetail Communi- cations, Hartford Design, Woz Design

0519
Art Directors
Ted Stoir, Tim

Hartford, David
Wozniak
Designers
Ted Stoir, Tim
Hartford, David
Wozniak
Client
Underwriters
Laboratories
Tools/Software/Platform
Adobe InDesign,
Adobe Illustrator,
Adobe Photoshop
Font
Akzidenz Grotesk

Duffy Singapore

0189
Art Director
Christopher Lee
Designer
Christopher Lee
Client
Designers
Association
Singapore
Tools/Software/Platform
Freehand, Adobe
Photoshop
Font
Trade Gothic

0222
Art Director
Christopher Lee
Designer
Christopher Lee
Client
Designers
Association
Singapore
Tools/Software/Platform
Freehand, Adobe
Photoshop

0518
Art Director
Christopher Lee
Designer
Christopher Lee
Client
Wizards of Light
Tools/Software/Platform
Freehand, Adobe
Photoshop
Font
Avant Garde Gothic,
Courier, Mrs. Eaves,
Times

0566
Art Director
Christopher Lee
Designers
Christopher Lee,
Cara, Kai, Larry,
Welping, Michelle
Tools/Software/Platform
Freehand, Adobe
Photoshop
Font
Trade Gothic

0616
Art Director
Christopher Lee
Designer
Christopher Lee,
Cara, Kai, Larry,
Welping, Michelle
Tools/Software/Platform
Freehand, Adobe
Photoshop
Font
Trade Gothic

0659

Art Director
Christopher Lee
Designer
Christopher Lee
Client
Wizards of Light
Tools/Software/Platform
**Freehand, Adobe
Photoshop**

0714
Art Director
Christopher Lee
Designer
Christopher Lee
Client
Wizards of Light
Tools/Software/Platform
**Freehand, Adobe
Photoshop**

Dulude

0071
Art Director
Denis Dulude
Designer
Denis Dulude
Client
Denis Dulude
Tools/Software/Platform
**Adobe Illustrator,
Adobe Photoshop,
iTunes**
Fonts
**Dulude/Magma,
Diesel (2 Rebels)**

0483
Art Director
Denis Dulude
Designer
Denis Dulude
Client
Denis Dulude
Tools/Software/Platform
**Adobe Illustrator,
Adobe Photoshop**

FontLab

0542
Art Director
Denis Dulude
Designer
Denis Dulude
Client
Pol Baril
Tools/Software/Platform
**Adobe InDesign,
Adobe Illustrator,
iTunes**

0543
Art Director
Denis Dulude
Designer
Denis Dulude
Client
Pol Baril
Tools/Software/Platform
**Adobe InDesign,
Adobe Illustrator,
iTunes**
Font
Times (customized)

0544
Art Director
Denis Dulude
Designer
Denis Dulude
Client
Pol Baril
Tools/Software/Platform
**Adobe InDesign,
Adobe Illustrator,
iTunes**
Font
Times (customized)

0545
Art Director
Denis Dulude
Designer
Denis Dulude
Client
Pol Baril
Tools/Software/Platform
**Adobe InDesign,
Adobe Illustrator,
iTunes**

0546
Art Director
Denis Dulude
Designer
Denis Dulude
Client
Pol Baril
Tools/Software/Platform
**Adobe InDesign,
Adobe Illustrator,
iTunes**
Font
Times (customized)

0547
Art Director
Denis Dulude
Designer
Denis Dulude
Client
Pol Baril
Tools/Software/Platform
**Adobe InDesign,
Adobe Illustrator,
iTunes**
Font
Times (customized)

0548
Art Director
Denis Dulude
Designer
Denis Dulude
Client
Pol Baril
Tools/Software/Platform
**Adobe InDesign,
Adobe Illustrator**
Font
**Trade Gothic
(customized)**

0549
Art Director
Denis Dulude
Designer
Denis Dulude
Client
Pol Baril
Tools/Software/Platform
**Adobe InDesign,
Adobe Photoshop,
iTunes**

0550
Art Director
Denis Dulude
Designer
Denis Dulude
Client
Pol Baril
Tools/Software/Platform
**Adobe InDesign,
Adobe Illustrator,
iTunes**

0551
Art Director
Denis Dulude
Designer
Denis Dulude
Client
Pol Baril
Tools/Software/Platform
**Adobe InDesign,
Adobe Illustrator,**

iTunes

0552
Art Director
Denis Dulude
Designer
Denis Dulude
Client
Pol Baril
Tools/Software/Platform
**Adobe InDesign,
Adobe Illustrator,
iTunes**

0553
Art Director
Denis Dulude
Designer
Denis Dulude
Client
Pol Baril
Tools/Software/Platform
**Adobe InDesign,
Adobe Illustrator,
iTunes**
Font
Times (customized)

0678
Art Director
Denis Dulude
Designer
Denis Dulude
Client
Pol Baril
Tools/Software/Platform
**Adobe InDesign,
Adobe Illustrator,
iTunes**
Font
Times (customized)

0696
Art Director
Denis Dulude
Designer
Denis Dulude
Client
**Choiniere
Photographe**
Tools/Software/Platform
**Adobe InDesign,
Adobe Illustrator**
Font
**Trade Gothic
(customized)**

0770
Art Director
Denis Dulude
Designer
Denis Dulude
Client
Denis Dulude
Tools/Software/Platform
**Adobe InDesign,
Adobe Photoshop,
iTunes**

0771
Art Director
Denis Dulude
Designer
Denis Dulude
Client
Denis Dulude
Tools/Software/Platform
**Adobe InDesign,
Adobe Photoshop,
iTunes**

0774
Art Director
Denis Dulude
Designer
Denis Dulude
Client
Denis Dulude
Tools/Software/Platform
**Adobe Illustrator,
Adobe Photoshop,
iTunes**

0841

Art Director
Denis Dulude
Designer
Denis Dulude
Client
Denis Dulude
Tools/Software/Platform
**Adobe Illustrator,
Adobe Photoshop,
iTunes**

0875
Art Director
Denis Dulude
Designer
Denis Dulude
Client
Denis Dulude
Tools/Software/Platform
**Adobe Illustrator,
Adobe Photoshop,
iTunes**

0989
Art Director
Denis Dulude
Designer
Denis Dulude
Client
Cité-Amerique
Tools/Software/Platform
**Adobe InDesign,
Adobe After Effects**
Font
**Trade Gothic
(customized)**

0990
Art Director
Denis Dulude
Designer
Denis Dulude
Client
Cité-Amerique
Tools/Software/Platform
**Adobe InDesign,
Adobe After Effects**
Font
**Trade Gothic
(customized)**

0991
Art Director
Denis Dulude
Designer
Denis Dulude
Client
Cité-Amerique
Tools/Software/Platform
**Adobe InDesign,
Adobe After Effects**
Font
**Trade Gothic
(customized)**

0992
Art Director
Denis Dulude
Designer
Denis Dulude
Client
Cité-Amerique
Tools/Software/Platform
**Adobe InDesign,
Adobe After Effects**
Font
**Trade Gothic
(customized)**

0998
Art Director
Denis Dulude
Designer
Denis Dulude
Client
Cité-Amerique
Tools/Software/Platform
**Adobe InDesign,
Adobe After Effects**
Font

Trade Gothic
(customized)

0999
Art Director
Denis Dulude
Designer
Denis Dulude
Client
Cité-Amerique
Tools/Software/Platform
**Adobe InDesign,
Adobe After Effects**
Font
**Trade Gothic
(customized)**

Eggers &
Diaper

0306
Art Director
Mark Diaper
Designer
Mark Diaper
Client
**Artangel/Public Art
Fund**

0695
Art Directors
**Birgit Eggers, Mark
Diaper**
Designers
**Birgit Eggers, Mark
Diaper**
Client
**European Space
Agency**

0736
Art Directors
**Birgit Eggers, Mark
Diaper**
Designers
**Birgit Eggers, Mark
Diaper**
Client
**European Space
Agency**

Elizabeth
Resnick
Design

0823
Art Director
Elizabeth Resnick
Designer
Elizabeth Resnick
Client
**Massachusetts
College of Art**
Tools/Software/Platform
QuarkXPress
Font
Martina, Galliard

elliottyoung

0400
Art Director
Dan Elliott
Designer
Dan Elliott
Client
Jet Couture

0463
Art Director
Dan Elliott
Designer
Dan Elliott
Client
Jet Couture

0465
Art Director
Dan Elliott

Designer
Dan Elliott
Client
Jet Couture

emeryfrost

0198
Designer
Emeryfrost
Client
Zembia

0208
Designer
Emeryfrost
Client
Zembia

0233
Designer
Emeryfrost
Client
Zembia

0259
Designer
Emeryfrost
Client
Zembia

0260
Designer
Emeryfrost
Client
Zembia

0262
Designer
Emeryfrost
Client
Zembia

0263
Designer
Emeryfrost
Client
Zembia

0287
Designer
Emeryfrost
Client
Zembia

0305
Designer
Emeryfrost
Client
Zembia

0313
Designer
Emeryfrost
Client
Zembia

0351
Designer
Emeryfrost
Client
Zembia

0352
Designer
Emeryfrost
Client
Zembia

0358
Designer
Emeryfrost
Client
Zembia

0359
Designer
Emeryfrost
Client
Zembia

Enspace, Inc.

0593
Designer
**Jenn Visocky
O'Grady, Ken
Visocky O'Grady,
Paul Perchinske**
Client
Solutions at Work
Tools/Software/Platform
**QuarkXPress, Adobe
Illustrator, Adobe
Photoshop,**
Fonts
**Franklin Gothic,
Centennial**

0594
Designer
**Jenn Visocky
O'Grady, Ken
Visocky O'Grady,
Paul Perchinske**
Client
Solutions at Work
Tools/Software/Platform
**QuarkXPress, Adobe
Illustrator, Adobe
Photoshop,**
Fonts
**Franklin Gothic,
Centennial**

0596
Designer
**Jenn Visocky
O'Grady, Ken
Visocky O'Grady,
Paul Perchinske**
Client
Solutions at Work
Tools/Software/Platform
**QuarkXPress, Adobe
Illustrator, Adobe
Photoshop,**
Fonts
**Franklin Gothic,
Centennial**

0817
Designer
**Jenn Visocky
O'Grady, Ken
Visocky O'Grady,
Paul Perchinske**
Client
**Cleveland Chamber
Symphony**
Tools/Software/Platform
**Adobe InDesign,
Adobe Illustrator,
Adobe Photoshop,**
Fonts
Trade Gothic

Envision+

0535
Designers
**Esther Mildenberger,
Brian Switzer**
Client
20/20 Media
Tools/Software/Platform
**Adobe Illustrator,
Adobe Photoshop**

0540
Designers
**Esther Mildenberger,
Brian Switzer**
Client
20/20 Media
Tools/Software/Platform
**Adobe Illustrator,
Adobe Photoshop**

0541
Designers

Esther Mildenberger,
Brian Switzer
Client
20/20 Media
Tools/Software/Platform
Adobe Illustrator,
Adobe Photoshop

0669
Designers
Esther Mildenberger,
Brian Switzer
Client
Interaction Design
Institute Ivrea
Tools/Software/Platform
QuarkXPress, Adobe
Illustrator, Adobe
Photoshop
Fonts
FF (sans), Bodoni

0856
Designer
Brian Switzer
Client
Interaction Design
Institute Ivrea
Tools/Software/Platform
QuarkXPress, Adobe
Photoshop
Fonts
FF (serif), FF Din

Felder
Grafikdesign
0526
Art Director
Peter Felder
Designers
Rene Dalpra. Peter
Felder
Client
Telefonseelsorge
Vorarlberg
Tools/Software/Platform
QuarkXPress
Paper/Materials
Elk Munken Offset,
150 gsm

0658
Art Director
Peter Felder
Client
Felder Grafikdesign
Tools/Software/Platform
QuarkXPress
Paper/Materials
Spoilage, waste-
paper

0661
Art Director
Peter Felder
Client
Felder Grafikdesign
Tools/Software/Platform
QuarkXPress
Fonts
Architype
Tschichold,
Augustea

0666
Art Director
Peter Felder
Client
Felder Grafikdesign
Tools/Software/Platform
QuarkXPress
Paper/Materials
Spoilage, waste-
paper

Felton
Communi-

cation
0892
Art Director
Brian Furnell
Client
Terrence Higgins
Trust
Tools/Software/Platform
QuarkXPress, Adobe
Photoshop
Paper/Materials
Challenger Offset,
vinyl

0896
Art Director
Brian Furnell
Client
Terrence Higgins
Trust
Tools/Software/Platform
QuarkXPress, Adobe
Photoshop
Paper/Materials
Challenger Offset,
vinyl

0921
Art Director
Brian Furnell
Client
Terrence Higgins
Trust
Tools/Software/Platform
QuarkXPress, Adobe
Photoshop
Paper/Materials
Challenger Offset,
vinyl

Form Fünf
Bremen
0036
Designer
Daniel Henry Bastian
Client
Form Fünf Bremen
Tools/Software/Platform
Freehand

Frida Larios
0820
Art Director
Frida Larios
Client
Frida Larios
Client
Self-initiated project
Tools/Software/Platform
Adobe Illustrator

Marino A.
Gallo
0386
Client
Polestar
Tools/Software/Platform
Adobe Illustrator,
Adobe Photoshop

0379
Client
Marino A. Gallo
Tools/Software/Platform
Adobe Illustrator,
Adobe Photoshop

0464
Client
Marino A. Gallo
Tools/Software/Platform
Adobe Illustrator,
Adobe Photoshop

0967
Client

Ogilvy & Mather
Tools/Software/Platform
Adobe Illustrator,
Adobe Photoshop

Gee & Chung
Design
0637
Art Director
Earl Gee
Designers
Earl Gee, Fani Chung
Client
DCM-Doll Capital
Management
Tools/Software/Platform
Adobe InDesign,
Adobe Illustrator,
Adobe Photoshop
Fonts
Adobe Garamond,
Trade Gothic

Gervais
0761
Art Director
Fran Gois Gervais
Designer
Fran Gois Gervais
Client
Fran Gois Gervais
Tools/Software/Platform
Adobe Photoshop

0797
Art Director
Jacqueline VD
Brugge
Designer
Jacqueline VD
Brugge
Client
In Discussion Right
Now (publisher)

0796
Art Director
Gervais
Designer
Gervais
Client
Papyrus Paper
Company NC

Ash Gibson
0229
Art Director
Ash Gibson
Designer
Ash Gibson
Client
Dennis Publishing
(UK)
Tools/Software/Platform
Adobe Illustrator,
Adobe Photoshop
Font
FJ Extended
(by Ash Gibson)

0310
Art Director
Ash Gibson
Designer
Ash Gibson
Client
Dennis Publishing
(UK)
Tools/Software/Platform
Adobe Illustrator,
Adobe Photoshop
Font
FJ Extended
(by Ash Gibson)

0311
Art Director

Ash Gibson
Designer
Ash Gibson
Client
Dennis Publishing
(UK)
Tools/Software/Platform
Adobe Illustrator,
Adobe Photoshop
Font
FJ Extended
(by Ash Gibson)

0350
Art Director
Ash Gibson
Designer
Ash Gibson
Client
Dennis Publishing
(UK)
Tools/Software/Platform
Adobe Illustrator,
Adobe Photoshop
Font
FJ Extended
(by Ash Gibson)

Giorgio
Davanzo
Design
0470
Art Director
Giorgio Davanzo
Designer
Giorgio Davanzo
Client
PD3
Tools/Software/Platform
QuarkXPress, Adobe
Illustrator
Font
Franklin Gothic

Gouthier
Design Inc.
0089
Art Director
Jonathon Gouthier
Designers
Jonathon Gouthier,
Kiley Del Valle
Client
Gouthier Design
Tools/Software/Platform
Adobe Photoshop,
Adobe Illustrator,
QuarkXPress
Paper/Materials
French Construction,
Stora Enso Centura

0171
Art Director
Jonathon Gouthier
Designers
Jonathon Gouthier,
Kiley Del Valle
Client
Gouthier Design
Tools/Software/Platform
Adobe Photoshop,
Adobe Illustrator,
QuarkXPress
Paper/Materials
French Construction,
Stora Enso Centura

0473
Art Director
Jonathon Gouthier
Designers
Jonathon Gouthier,
Kiley Del Valle
Client
Gouthier Design
Tools/Software/Platform

Adobe Photoshop,
Adobe Illustrator,
QuarkXPress
Paper/Materials
French Construction,
Stora Enso Centura

0732
Art Director
Jonathon Gouthier
Designers
Jonathon Gouthier,
Kiley Del Valle
Client
Ad Fed of Greater
Fort Lauderdale
Tools/Software/Platform
Adobe Illustrator,
QuarkXPress
Paper/Materials
Epson high quality
inkjet French con-
struction

Graphiculture
0001
Art Director
Chad Olson
Client
Ann E. Cutting
Tools/Software/Platform
Quark
Font
Clarendon

0005
Art Director
Chad Olson
Client
Ann E. Cutting
Tools/Software/Platform
QuarkXPress
Font
Clarendon

0177
Art Director
Chad Olson
Client
Ann E. Cutting
Tools/Software/Platform
Quark
Font
Clarendon

Groothuis &
Malsy
0223
Art Directors
Victor Malsy,
Gilmar Wendt
Designer
Gilmar Wendt
Client
Groothuis & Malsy
Tools/Software/Platform
QuarkXPress
Paper/Materials
Schleipen Fly,
Rainbow Rosebud

0227
Art Directors
Victor Malsy,
Gilmar Wendt
Designer
Gilmar Wendt
Client
Groothuis & Malsy
Tools/Software/Platform
QuarkXPress
Paper/Materials
Schleipen Fly,
Rainbow Rosebud

0264
Art Directors
Victor Malsy,

Gilmar Wendt
Designer
Gilmar Wendt
Client
Groothuis & Malsy
Tools/Software/Platform
QuarkXPress
Paper/Materials
Schleipen Fly,
Rainbow Rosebud

0342
Art Directors
Victor Malsy,
Gilmar Wendt
Designer
Gilmar Wendt
Client
Groothuis & Malsy
Tools/Software/Platform
QuarkXPress
Paper/Materials
Schleipen Fly,
Rainbow Rosebud

0362
Art Directors
Victor Malsy,
Gilmar Wendt
Designer
Gilmar Wendt
Client
Groothuis & Malsy
Tools/Software/Platform
QuarkXPress
Paper/Materials
Schleipen Fly,
Rainbow Rosebud

Guru Design
0587
Art Director
Claus Rysser
Designer
Claus Rysser
Client
Guru Design
Tools/Software/Platform
Adobe Photoshop,
Adobe Illustrator
Fonts
Helvetica Neue,
Haetenschweiller,
Verdana

0589
Art Director
Claus Rysser
Designer
Claus Rysser
Client
Guru Design
Tools/Software/Platform
Adobe Photoshop,
Adobe Illustrator
Fonts
Helvetica Neue,
Haetenschweiller,
Verdana

0590
Art Director
Claus Rysser
Designer
Claus Rysser
Client
Guru Design
Tools/Software/Platform
Adobe Photoshop,
Adobe Illustrator
Fonts
Helvetica Neue,
Haetenschweiller,
Verdana

0618
Art Director
Claus Rysser
Designer

Claus Rysser
Client
Guru Design
Tools/Software/Platform
Adobe Photoshop,
Adobe Illustrator
Fonts
Helvetica Neue,
Haetenschweiller,
Verdana

0621
Art Director
Claus Rysser
Designer
Claus Rysser
Client
Guru Design
Tools/Software/Platform
Adobe Photoshop,
Adobe Illustrator
Fonts
Helvetica Neue,
Haetenschweiller,
Verdana

0693
Art Director
Claus Rysser
Designer
Claus Rysser
Client
Guru Design
Tools/Software/Platform
Adobe Photoshop,
Adobe Illustrator
Fonts
Helvetica Neue,
Haetenschweiller,
Verdana

H2D2, Visual
Communi-
cations
0083
Art Director
Markus Remscheid
Client
Self Promotion
Tools/Software/Platform
Freehand, Adobe
Photoshop
Font
H2D2-Flame

Harcus Design
0186
Art Director
Annette Harcus
Designer
Phoebe Besley
Client
John Guthrie
Tools/Software/Platform
Adobe Illustrator,
Adobe Photoshop
Font
Rosewood-Fill

0398
Art Director
Annette Harcus
Designers
Melonie Ryan,
Annette Harcus
Client
Arinya Accessories
Tools/Software/Platform
Adobe Illustrator
Fonts
Futura, hand drawn

0497
Art Director
Annette Harcus
Designer
Marianne Walter
Client

Man Investments
Tools/Software/Platform
Adobe Illustrator,
Adobe Photoshop,
QuarkXPress
Font
Helvetica Neue

0563
Art Director
Annette Harcus
Designer
Marianne Walter
Client
Man Investments
Tools/Software/Platform
Adobe Illustrator,
Adobe Photoshop,
QuarkXPress
Font
Helvetica Neue

0619
Art Director
Annette Harcus
Designer
Melonie Ryan,
Annette Harcus
Client
Yalumba Wine
Company
Tools/Software/Platform
Adobe Illustrator,
Adobe Photoshop,
QuarkXPress
Fonts
Bodoni Antiqua,
Helvetica Neue

0905
Art Director
Annette Harcus
Designer
Phoebe Besley
Client
The Evans Wine
Company
Tools/Software/Platform
Adobe Illustrator,
Adobe Photoshop
Font
Trajan

0908
Art Director
Annette Harcus
Designer
Melonie Ryan,
Annette Harcus
Client
Yalumba Wine
Company
Tools/Software/Platform
Adobe Illustrator
Font
Serlio

Harrimansteel

0776
Art Director
Harrimansteel
Designer
Harrimansteel
Client
First Impression Ltd.
Tools/Software/Platform
Adobe Illustrator
Fonts
Illustrator Swiss,
Helvetica Neue

0779
Art Director
Harrimansteel
Designer
Harrimansteel
Client
First Impression Ltd.
Tools/Software/Platform

Adobe Illustrator
Fonts
Illustrator Swiss,
Helvetica Neue

0782
Art Director
Harrimansteel
Designer
Harrimansteel
Client
First Impression Ltd.
Tools/Software/Platform
Adobe Illustrator
Fonts
Illustrator Swiss,
Helvetica Neue

0821
Art Director
Harrimansteel
Designer
Harrimansteel
Client
Hurley International
Paper/Materials
Tracing paper
and pen
Font
Hand drawn

Hartford Design

0369
Art Director
Tim Hartford
Designer
Ron Alikpala
Client
Wishbpne
Restaurant
Tools/Software/Platform
QuarkXPress, Adobe
Illustrator, Adobe
Photoshop
Font
Customized

0444
Art Director
Tim Hartford
Designer
Hartford Design
Tools/Software/Platform
QuarkXPress, Adobe
Illustrator
Font
Seria Sans

0493
Art Director
Tim Hartford
Designer
Tim Hartford
Client
Jessica Tampas
Photography
Tools/Software/Platform
QuarkXPress, Adobe
Illustrator
Font
OCRA

0527
Art Director
Tim Hartford
Designer
Tim Hartford
Client
Marc Hauser
Photography,
Nimrod Systems
Tools/Software/Platform
QuarkXPress, Adobe
Illustrator, Adobe
Photoshop
Fonts

**Clarendon, Trade
Gothic**

0522
Art Director
Tim Hartford
Designer
Ron Alikpala
Client
American Dietetic
Association
Tools/Software/Platform
QuarkXPress, Adobe
Illustrator, Adobe
Photoshop
Font
Trade Gothic, Adobe
Garamond

0534
Art Director
Tim Hartford
Designer
Tim Hartford
Client
Jessica Tampas
Photography
Tools/Software/Platform
QuarkXPress, Adobe
Illustrator

0595
Art Director
Tim Hartford
Designer
Tim Hartford
Client
Marc Hauser
Photography,
Nimrod Systems
Tools/Software/Platform
QuarkXPress, Adobe
Illustrator, Adobe
Photoshop
Font

0614
Art Director
Tim Hartford
Designer
Tim Hartford
Client
American Dietetic
Association
Tools/Software/Platform
QuarkXPress, Adobe
Illustrator, Adobe
Photoshop
Font
Helvetica Neue

0630
Art Director
Tim Hartford
Designer
Tim Hartford
Client
Marc Hauser
Photography,
Nimrod Systems
Tools/Software/Platform
QuarkXPress, Adobe
Illustrator, Adobe
Photoshop

0631
Art Director
Tim Hartford
Designer
Tim Hartford
Client
Marc Hauser
Photography,
Nimrod Systems
Tools/Software/Platform
QuarkXPress, Adobe
Illustrator, Adobe
Photoshop

0674

Art Director
Tim Hartford
Designer
Tim Hartford
Client
American Dietetic
Association
Tools/Software/Platform
QuarkXPress, Adobe
Illustrator, Adobe
Photoshop

0729
Art Director
Tim Hartford
Designer
Tim Hartford
Client
Bill Tucker, Nimrod
Systems
Tools/Software/Platform
QuarkXPress, Adobe
Photoshop
Font
Trade Gothic

Heckman

0098
Art Director
Denise Heckman
Designer
Denise Heckman
Client
Syracuse University
Tools/Software/Platform
Quark, Adobe
Photoshop, Adobe
Illustrator/Mac
Fonts
Akzidenz Grotesk,
Garamond

0100
Art Director
Denise Heckman
Designer
Denise Heckman
Client
Syracuse University
Tools/Software/Platform
QuarkXPress, Adobe
Photoshop, Adobe
Illustrator/Mac
Fonts
Andale Mono,
Akzidenz Grotesk,
Times

Hornall Anderson Design Works, Inc.

0426
Art Directors
James Tee, John
Anicker
Designers
James Tee, Elmer
dela Cruz, Kris
Delaney
Client
Zango
Tools/Software/Platform
Freehand

0436
Art Director
Jack Anderson
Designers
Jack Anderson,
Andrew Wicklund,
Mark Popich, Henry
Yiu, Lauren DiRusso,
Ed Lee
Client
Seattle SuperSonics
Tools/Software/Platform

QuarkXPress, Adobe
Photoshop

0567
Art Director
Jack Anderson
Designers
Jack Anderson,
Andrew Wicklund,
Mark Popich, Henry
Yiu, Lauren DiRusso,
Ed Lee
Client
Seattle SuperSonics
Tools/Software/Platform
QuarkXPress, Adobe
Photoshop

0568
Art Director
Jack Anderson
Designers
Jack Anderson,
Andrew Wicklund,
Mark Popich, Henry
Yiu, Lauren DiRusso,
Ed Lee
Client
Seattle SuperSonics
Tools/Software/Platform
QuarkXPress, Adobe
Photoshop

0569
Art Director
Jack Anderson
Designers
Jack Anderson,
Elmer dela Cruz,
Henry Yiu, Belinda
Bowling, Jay Hilburn,
Beckon Wyld, Jeff
Wolff
Client
Washington Wizards
Tools/Software/Platform
QuarkXPress, Adobe
Photoshop

0570
Art Director
Jack Anderson
Designer
Jack Anderson,
Andrew Wicklund,
Mark Popich, Henry
Yiu, Lauren DiRusso,
Ed Lee
Client
Seattle SuperSonics
Tools/Software/Platform
QuarkXPress, Adobe
Photoshop

0571
Art Director
Jack Anderson
Designers
Jack Anderson,
Elmer dela Cruz,
Henry Yiu, Belinda
Bowling, Jay Hilburn,
Beckon Wyld, Jeff
Wolff
Client
Washington Wizards
Tools/Software/Platform
QuarkXPress, Adobe
Photoshop

0911
Art Director
Jack Anderson
Designers
Jack Anderson,
Sonja Max, James
Tee, Tiffany Place,
Elmer dela Cruz,
Jana Nishi

QuarkXPress, Adobe
Photoshop

0920
Art Directors
Jack Anderson, Larry
Anderson
Designers
Larry Anderson,
Elmer dela Cruz,
Bruce Stigler, Jay
Hilburn, Dorothee
Soechting, Don
Stayner
Client
Widmer Brothers
Tools/Software/Platform

0922
Art Director
Jack Anderson
Designers
Jack Anderson,
Andrew Wicklund,
Henry Yiu, Andrew
Smith, Bruce
Branson-Meyer,
John Anderle
Client
PMI

Hoyne Design

0399
Art Director
Andrew Hoyne
Designer
Andrew Hoyne
Client
Schiavello
Tools/Software/Platform
Adobe Illustrator
Font
Hand drawn

0894
Art Director
Andrew Hoyne
Designer
James West
Client
BMG Music Australia
Tools/Software/Platform
QuarkXPress, Adobe
Photoshop, Adobe
Illustrator
Fonts
Mrs. Eaves, Helvetica
Neue, hand drawn

0965
Art Director
Andrew Hoyne
Designer
James West
Client
Nike Australia
Tools/Software/Platform
Adobe Illustrator
Font
Hand drawn

0968
Art Director
Andrew Hoyne
Designer
James West
Client
Nike Australia
Tools/Software/Platform
Adobe Illustrator
Font
Hand drawn

0982
Art Director
Andrew Hoyne
Designers
Andrew Hoyne, David

Marinelli
Client
Il Fornalo
Tools/Software/Platform
Adobe Illustrator,
Adobe Photoshop
Font
Hand drawn

IAAH/iamalwayshungry

0138
Art Director
Nessim Higson
Designers
Nessim Higson,
Chuck Wooding
Client
Self promotion,
Chuck Wooding
Tools/Software/Platform
QuarkXPress, Adobe
Illustrator, Adobe
Photoshop
Fonts
Mrs. Eaves, Helvetica
Neue Condensed

0167
Art Director
Nessim Higson
Designer
Nessim Higson
Client
Self promotion,
personal
Tools/Software/Platform
Quark, Adobe
Illustrator
Font
Didot

0731
Art Director
Nessim Higson
Designer
Nessim Higson
Client
Self promotion, IAAH
Tools/Software/Platform
Adobe Photoshop
Fonts
Mrs. Eaves, Didot

0778
Art Director
Nessim Higson
Designer
Nessim Higson
Client
AIGA Birmingham
Tools/Software/Platform
Adobe Illustrator
Fonts
Futura, Knockout,
Rosewood, Decolade

0933
Art Director
Nessim Higson
Designer
Nessim Higson
Client
Genex
Tools/Software/Platform
Adobe Photoshop,
Adobe Illustrator
Fonts
HTF Knockout,
Helvetica, Clarendon

Ideation Signs & Communications, Inc.

0011
Art Director
Kacha Azema

Designer
Kacha Azema
Client
Rustproof Youth Ministries
Tools/Software/Platform
Adobe Illustrator/ Mac OS
Fonts
Hand drawn, custom

0012
Art Director
Kacha Azema
Designer
Kacha Azema
Client
Rustproof Youth Ministries
Tools/Software/Platform
Adobe Illustrator/ Mac OS
Fonts
Hand drawn, custom

0013
Art Director
Kacha Azema
Designer
Kacha Azema
Client
Rustproof Youth Ministries
Tools/Software/Platform
Adobe Illustrator/ Mac OS
Fonts
Hand drawn, custom

Insight Design Communications

0143
Art Director
Tracy Holdeman
Designer
Lea Carmichael
Client
YAAA
Tools/Software/Platform
Freehand
Fonts
Badhouse, Alternate Gothic

0814
Art Director
Tracy Holderman
Designer
Lea Carmichael
Client
Public Relations Society of America
Tools/Software/Platform
Freehand, Adobe Photoshop
Fonts
Redfive, Robotik, Epokha, P22 Sinel

Yanek Iontef

0033
Art Director
Yanek Iontef
Designer
Yanek Iontef
Client
Yanek Iontef
Tools/Software/Platform
Macromedia Fontographer, Freehand
Font
Erica Sans (Hebrew – light, medium, bold)

0034
Art Director

Art Director
Yanek Iontef
Designer
Yanek Iontef
Client
Pauza Products and Services Ltd.
Tools/Software/Platform
Macromedia Fontographer, Freehand
Font
Pauza (Hebrew and Latin – light, medium, bold, black)

0240
Art Director
Yanek Iontef
Designer
Yanek Iontef
Client
FSI–Font Shop International
Tools/Software/Platform
Freehand
Font
FF Cartonnage-Alternate, Roman, Pict

0241
Art Director
Yanek Iontef
Designer
Yanek Iontef
Client
FSI–Font Shop International
Tools/Software/Platform
Freehand
Font
FF Cartonnage-Alternate, Roman, Pict

0242
Art Director
Yanek Iontef
Designer
Yanek Iontef
Client
FSI–Font Shop International
Tools/Software/Platform
Freehand
Font
FF Cartonnage-Alternate, Roman, Pict

0243
Art Director
Yanek Iontef
Designer
Yanek Iontef
Client
FSI–Font Shop International
Tools/Software/Platform
Freehand
Font
FF Cartonnage-Alternate, Roman, Pict

0244
Art Director
Yanek Iontef
Designer
Yanek Iontef
Client
FSI–Font Shop International
Tools/Software/Platform
Freehand
Font
FF Cartonnage-Alternate, Roman, Pict

0245
Art Director
Yanek Iontef
Designer
Yanek Iontef
Client
FSI–Font Shop International
Tools/Software/Platform
Freehand
Font
FF Cartonnage-Alternate, Roman, Pict

0246
Art Director
Yanek Iontef
Designer
Yanek Iontef
Client
FSI–Font Shop International
Tools/Software/Platform
Freehand
Font
FF Cartonnage-Alternate, Roman, Pict

0412
Art Director
Yanek Iontef
Designer
Yanek Iontef
Client
FSI–Font Shop International
Tools/Software/Platform
Freehand
Font
FF Cartonnage-Alternate, Roman, Pict

0789
Art Director
Yanek Iontef
Designer
Yanek Iontef
Client
GESHER Theatre (Russian and Hebrewspeaking theatre)
Tools/Software/Platform
Freehand, Adobe Photoshop
Fonts
Helvetica (Cyrillic), Nakris Tam (Hebrew)

0873
Art Director
Yanek Iontef
Designer
Yanek Iontef
Client
Tel Aviv Museum of Art
Tools/Software/Platform
Freehand, Adobe Photoshop
Fonts
Bell Gothic (Latin), Haim (Hebrew)

IRBE Design

0772
Art Director
Igors Irbe
Client
IRBE Design
Tools/Software/Platform
QuarkXPress, Adobe Photoshop
Paper/Materials
Gilbert Clear Vellum

---

iridium, a design agency

0717
Art Directors
Jean-Luc Denat, Mario L'Ecuyer
Designer
Mario L'Ecuyer
Client
Mitel Corporation
Tools/Software/Platform
QuarkXPress, Adobe Photoshop
Paper/Materials
Graphika Lineal, Potlatch McCoy Gloss, French Paper Construction

0744
Art Director
Etienne Bessette
Designer
Etienne Bessette
Client
Epsilon
Tools/Software/Platform
QuarkXPress, Adobe Illustrator, Adobe Photoshop
Paper/Materials
Sappi Horizon Silk

Iron Design

0137
Art Director
Todd Edmunds
Designer
Xanthe Matychak
Client
Iron Design
Tools/Software/Platform
Adobe Illustrator
Fonts
Helvetica, Signpainter Family

0842
Art Director
Todd Edmunds
Designer
Louis Johnson
Client
AIDS Work (Southern Tier AIDS Program)
Tools/Software/Platform
Adobe Photoshop, Adobe Illustrator
Fonts
Clarendon, Parapa Display Caps, Poplar Black, Vingta, Runic, Slot Ssk

Jan Family

0067
Designer
Soffi Beier
Font
Based on Helvetica Neue

0072
Designer
Soffi Beier
Font
Based on Helvetica Neue

0220
Designer
Soffi Beier
Font
Based on Helvetica Neue

0254

Designer
Soffi Beier
Font
Based on Helvetica Neue

0255
Designer
Soffi Beier
Font
Based on Helvetica Neue

0258
Designer
Soffi Beier
Font
Based on Helvetica Neue

Jason Gomez

0097
Art Director
Jason Gomez
Designer
Jason Gomez
Client
Joanna Schulz
Tools/Software/Platform
Adobe Illustrator, Adobe Photoshop/ Mac
Fonts
Bickham Script, Bembo Expert, customized

Joe Miller's Company

0004
Designer
Joe Miller
Client
Works/San Jose
Tools/Software/Platform
Adobe Photoshop, QuarkXPress
Font
Akzidenz Grotesk

0096
Designer
Joe Miller
Client
Works/San Jose
Tools/Software/Platform
Adobe Photoshop, QuarkXPress/Mac
Fonts
Didot, Bauer Bodoni

0368
Designer
Joe Miller
Client
Works/San Jose
Tools/Software/Platform
Adobe Illustrator, Adobe Photoshop, QuarkXPress

0442
Designer
Joe Miller
Client
Poetry Center San Jose
Tools/Software/Platform
Adobe Illustrator
Fonts
Mrs. Eaves, Helvetica, Times, customized

0525
Designer
Joe Miller
Client

Designer
Soffi Beier
Font
Based on Helvetica Neue
Fonts
Akzidenz Grotesk

0773
Designer
Joe Miller
Client
Works/San Jose
Tools/Software/Platform
Adobe Photoshop, Adobe Illustrator
Font
Helvetica

0838
Designer
Joe Miller
Client
Works/San Jose
Tools/Software/Platform
Adobe Photoshop, QuarkXPress
Fonts
Baskerville, Akzidenz Grotesk

0839
Designer
Joe Miller
Client
Works/San Jose
Tools/Software/Platform
Adobe Illustrator, QuarkXPress
Fonts
Stroke, Century

0854
Designer
Joe Miller
Client
Works/San Jose
Tools/Software/Platform
Adobe Photoshop, Adobe Photoshop, Streamline, QuarkXPress
Fonts
Presstype, hand drawn

0880
Designer
Joe Miller
Client
Works/San Jose
Tools/Software/Platform
Adobe Photoshop, Adobe Illustrator, QuarkXPress
Fonts
Akzidenz Grotesk

Johann A. Gomez

0401
Art Director
Johann A. Gomez
Designer
Johann A. Gomez
Client
Replicant Wear
Tools/Software/Platform
Adobe Illustrator, Adobe Photoshop
Font
Customized

0431
Art Director
Johann A. Gomez
Designer
Johann A. Gomez
Client

Association for Viet Arts
Tools/Software/Platform
Adobe Photoshop, QuarkXPress
Fonts
Akzidenz Grotesk

Microsoft
Tools/Software/Platform
Adobe Illustrator, Adobe Photoshop
Font
Customized

0461
Art Director
Johann A. Gomez
Designer
Johann A. Gomez
Client
Black Panties
Tools/Software/Platform
Adobe Illustrator, Freehand, Adobe Photoshop
Font
Customized

Johnson Banks

0190
Art Director
Michael Johnson
Designers
Julia Woollams, Kater Hudball
Client
Conran Octopus
Tools/Software/Platform
QuarkXPress
Paper/Materials
Cloth, machine

0224
Art Director
Michael Johnson
Designers
Julia Woollams, Kater Hudball
Client
Conran Octopus
Tools/Software/Platform
QuarkXPress
Paper/Materials
Cloth, machine

Jones Design Group

0104
Art Director
Vicky Jones
Designer
Katherine Staggs, Brody Boye
Client
Jones Dsign Group
Tools/Software/Platform
QuarkXPress, Adobe Illustrator
Paper/Materials
Tattoos

Juan Torneros

0791
Art Director
Juan Torneros
Designer
Juan Torneros
Client
Universidad Nacional de Columbia
Tools/Software/Platform
Freehand, Adobe Photoshop
Font
TV Screen Fonts, Zurich

0826
Art Director
Juan Torneros
Designer
Juan Torneros
Client

Universidad Nacional de Columbia
Tools/Software/Platform
Freehand, Adobe Photoshop
Fonts
TV Screen Fonts, Zurich

0882
Art Director
Juan Torneros
Designer
Juan Torneros
Client
Universidad Nacional de Columbia
Tools/Software/Platform
Freehand, Adobe Photoshop
Fonts
TV Screen Fonts, Zurich

Juicy Temples Creative
0370
Art Director
Klaus Heesch
Designers
Randy J. Hunt, Ross Pike
Client
Juicy Temples Creative
Tools/Software/Platform
Adobe Illustrator
Font
CA Aires

0404
Art Director
Klaus Heesch
Designers
Randy J. Hunt, Ross Pike
Client
Juicy Temples Creative
Tools/Software/Platform
Adobe Illustrator

0957
Art Director
Klaus Heesch
Designer
Anthony DeLaura, Randy J. Hunt
Client
Juicy Temples Creative
Tools/Software/Platform
Flash, Adobe Illustrator
Fonts
CA Aires, Urban, Mini

0958
Art Director
Klaus Heesch
Designer
Anthony DeLaura, Randy J. Hunt
Client
Juicy Temples Creative
Tools/Software/Platform
Flash, Adobe Illustrator

0959
Art Director
Klaus Heesch
Designer
Anthony DeLaura, Randy J. Hunt
Client
Juicy Temples Creative

Flash, Adobe Illustrator

0960
Art Director
Klaus Heesch
Designer
Anthony DeLaura, Randy J. Hunt
Client
Juicy Temples Creative
Tools/Software/Platform
Flash, Adobe Illustrator

Karim Rashid Inc.
0433
Art Director
Valeria Bianco
Designer
Karim Rashid, Valeria Bianco
Tools/Software/Platform
Solidworks, Formz, Adobe Photoshop, Adobe Illustrator

0434
Art Director
Valeria Bianco
Designer
Karim Rashid, Valeria Bianco
Tools/Software/Platform
Solidworks, Formz, Adobe Photoshop, Adobe Illustrator

0437
Art Director
Valeria Bianco
Designer
Karim Rashid, Valeria Bianco
Tools/Software/Platform
Solidworks, Formz, Adobe Photoshop, Adobe Illustrator

0441
Art Director
Valeria Bianco
Designer
Karim Rashid, Valeria Bianco
Tools/Software/Platform
Solidworks, Formz, Adobe Photoshop, Adobe Illustrator

Kearney Rocholl Corporate Communications AG
0390
Art Director
Frank Rocholl
Designer
Frank Rocholl
Client
Vividrprojects GmbH
Tools/Software/Platform
Freehand
Font
Platelet

0391
Art Director
Frank Rocholl
Designer
Frank Rocholl
Client

Hype Magazine
Tools/Software/Platform
Freehand
Font
FF Jigger

0392
Art Director
Frank Rocholl
Designer
Frank Rocholl
Client
DBV Winterthur Versicherung
Tools/Software/Platform
Freehand
Font
Digital

0393
Art Director
Frank Rocholl
Designer
Frank Rocholl
Client
I-TV-T AG
Tools/Software/Platform
Freehand
Font
Bell Gothic, OCRA

0394
Art Director
Frank Rocholl
Designer
Frank Rocholl
Client
Audi AG
Tools/Software/Platform
Freehand
Font
Univers (Extended)

0395
Art Director
Frank Rocholl
Designer
Frank Rocholl
Client
Area Project Development Ltd., London
Tools/Software/Platform
Freehand
Fonts
Sackers Gothic, Officina

0718
Art Director
Frank Rocholl
Designer
Dmitri Lavrow
Client
Moller Design
Tools/Software/Platform
QuarkXPress
Font
Typestar

0719
Art Director
Frank Rocholl
Designer
Frank Rocholl
Client
Prof. Tom Philipps/ Rocholl Projects Folder
Tools/Software/Platform
Freehand
Font
Univers (Condensed)

0720
Art Director
Frank Rocholl
Designer
Dmitri Lavrow
Client

Moller Design
Tools/Software/Platform
QuarkXPress
Font
Typestar

0721
Art Director
Frank Rocholl
Designer
Frank Rocholl
Client
Area Project Development Ltd., London
Tools/Software/Platform
Freehand, Adobe Photoshop
Font
FF Jigger

0722
Art Director
Frank Rocholl
Designer
Michael Schmidt
Client
Hype Magazine
Tools/Software/Platform
Freehand, Adobe Photoshop
Font
FF Jigger, Pastelaria

0737
Art Director
Frank Rocholl
Designer
Frank Rocholl
Client
Kearney Rocholl
Tools/Software/Platform
Freehand
Font
Nuri (by Frank Rocholl)

0824
Art Director
Frank Rocholl
Designer
Frank Rocholl
Client
FH Darmstadt University of Applied Science
Tools/Software/Platform
Freehand, Adobe Photoshop
Font
Signature Development (head-line), FF Hardcase (copy)

0837
Art Director
Frank Rocholl
Designer
Frank Rocholl
Client
Levi Straus Germany
Tools/Software/Platform
Freehand
Font
Avante Garde, Franklin Gothic, Decorated, Astonished, Boomshaker

0840
Art Director
Frank Rocholl
Designer
Frank Rocholl
Client
Levi Straus Germany
Tools/Software/Platform
Freehand

Font
Avante Garde, Franklin Gothic, Decorated, Astonished, Boomshaker

0859
Art Director
Frank Rocholl
Designer
Frank Rocholl
Client
Levi Straus Germany
Tools/Software/Platform
Freehand
Font
Avante Garde, Franklin Gothic, Decorated, Astonished, Boomshaker

0861
Art Director
Frank Rocholl
Designer
Frank Rocholl
Client
Kearney Rocholl
Tools/Software/Platform
Freehand
Font
Nuri (by Frank Rocholl)

0862
Art Director
Frank Rocholl
Designer
Frank Rocholl
Client
Levi Straus Germany
Tools/Software/Platform
Freehand
Font
Avante Garde, Franklin Gothic, Decorated, Astonished, Boomshaker

0860
Art Director
Frank Rocholl
Designer
Frank Rocholl
Client
Levi Straus Germany
Tools/Software/Platform
Freehand
Font
Avante Garde, Franklin Gothic, Decorated, Astonished, Boomshaker

0885
Art Director
Frank Rocholl
Designer
Michael Schmidt
Client
Dittmar GmbH & Co. KG
Tools/Software/Platform
Freehand, Adobe Photoshop
Font
Dirty Ego, Diesel, Orator

0999
Art Director
Frank Rocholl
Designer
Heiko Gimbel
Client
Rocholl Projects

Font
Avante Garde, Franklin Gothic, Decorated, Astonished, Boomshaker

0879 [*reading: 0859 repeated? actual:*]
Tools/Software/Platform
Freehand, Adobe Photoshop, Flash, Dreamweaver
Fonts
News Gothic, Schild 7

1000
Art Director
Frank Rocholl
Designer
Heiko Gimbel
Client
Rocholl Projects
Tools/Software/Platform
Freehand, Adobe Photoshop, Flash, Dreamweaver
Font
News Gothic, Schild 7

Kessels Kramer
0701
Art Director
Erik Kessels

Kinetic Singapore
0446
Art Directors
Pann Lim, Leng Soh, Roy Poh
Designers
Pann Lim, Leng Soh, Roy Poh
Client
Kinetic Singapore
Tools/Software/Platform
Freehand
Paper/Materials
Woodfree Paper

Kolegram Design
0075
Art Director
Mike Teixeira
Designer
Mike Teixeira
Client
Kolegram Design
Tools/Software/Platform
QuarkXPress

Kontour Design
0103
Art Director
Sibylle Hagmann
Designer
Sibylle Hagmann
Client
Museum of Fine Arts - Houston, USA
Tools/Software/Platform
Adobe InDesign/Mac
Fonts
Council, Tarzana

0228
Art Director
Sibylle Hagmann
Designer
Sibylle Hagmann
Client
Dallas Museum of Art, USA
Tools/Software/Platform
QuarkXPress
Fonts
Dalliance, Foundry Gridnik

0279
Art Director
Sibylle Hagmann
Designer
Sibylle Hagmann
Client
Dallas Museum of Art, USA
Tools/Software/Platform
QuarkXPress

0633
Art Director
Sibylle Hagmann
Designer
Sibylle Hagmann
Client
Museum of Fine Arts Houston, USA
Tools/Software/Platform
Adobe InDesign
Fonts
Council, Brea

0634
Art Director
Sibylle Hagmann
Designer
Sibylle Hagmann
Client
Emigré, Sacramento, CA
Tools/Software/Platform
QuarkXPress
Font
Cholla

Kontrapunkt
0144
Art Director
Peter Van Toorn Brix
Designers
Bo Linnemann, Peter Van Toorn Brix
Client
Billund Airport
Tools/Software/Platform
Adobe Illustrator, Fontographer
Font
Customized

0406
Art Director
Eduard Cehovin
Designer
Eduard Cehovin
Client
Ivana Wineham
Tools/Software/Platform
A1

0407
Art Director
Peter Van Toorn Brix
Designer
Morten Sornsen, Peter Van Toorn Brix
Client
Semler

0408
Art Director
Bo Linnermann
Designers
Bo Linnermann
Client
Dansre Bank

KOREK Studio
0377
Art Director
Wojtek Koruc
KOREK
Designer
Wojtek Koruc
KOREK
Client
Transforma Ltd.

Tools/Software/Platform
Collage, Adobe Photoshop
Fonts
Helvetica, Acculs

KROG

0684
Art Director
Edi Berk
Designer
Edi Berk
Client
Obrtna zbornica Slovenije, Ljubljana
Tools/Software/Platform
QuarkXPress, Adobe Illustrator, Adobe Photoshop
Fonts
Garamond ITC, Franklin

Ligalux GmbH

0124
Art Directors
Petra Matouschek, Martina Massong
Designers
Martina Massong, Vicky Abndt
Client
Fischer Appelt Kommunikation, GmbH
Tools/Software/Platform
QuarkXPress, Freehand
Fonts
DTL Elzevire, Helvetica Neue

0169
Art Directors
Petra Matouschek, Martina Massong
Designers
Martina Massong, Vicky Abndt
Client
Fischer Appelt Kommunikation, GmbH
Tools/Software/Platform
QuarkXPress, Freehand
Fonts
DTL Elzevire, Helvetica Neue

0207
Art Director
Claudia Fischer-Appel
Designers
Claudia Fischer-Appel, Lars Nieb
Client
Ligalux GmbH
Tools/Software/Platform
Freehand
Paper/Materials
Munken & Luxomagi

0318
Art Director
Claudia Fischer-Appel
Designers
Claudia Fischer-Appel, Lars Nieb
Client
Ligalux GmbH
Tools/Software/Platform
Freehand
Paper/Materials
Munken & Luxomagi

0325

Art Director
Claudia Fischer-Appel
Designers
Claudia Fischer-Appel, Lars Nieb
Client
Ligalux GmbH
Tools/Software/Platform
Freehand
Paper/Materials
Munken & Luxomagi

0319
Art Director
Claudia Fischer-Appel
Designers
Claudia Fischer-Appel, Lars Nieb
Client
Ligalux GmbH
Tools/Software/Platform
Freehand
Paper/Materials
Munken & Luxomagi

0326
Art Director
Claudia Fischer-Appel
Designers
Claudia Fischer-Appel, Lars Nieb
Client
Ligalux GmbH
Tools/Software/Platform
Freehand
Paper/Materials
Munken & Luxomagi

0327
Art Director
Claudia Fischer-Appel
Designers
Claudia Fischer-Appel, Lars Nieb
Client
Ligalux GmbH
Tools/Software/Platform
Freehand
Paper/Materials
Munken & Luxomagi

0334
Art Director
Claudia Fischer-Appel
Designers
Claudia Fischer-Appel, Lars Nieb
Client
Ligalux GmbH
Tools/Software/Platform
Freehand
Paper/Materials
Munken & Luxomagi

0335
Art Director
Claudia Fischer-Appel
Designers
Claudia Fischer-Appel, Lars Nieb
Client
Ligalux GmbH
Tools/Software/Platform
Freehand
Paper/Materials
Munken & Luxomagi

0336
Art Director
Claudia Fischer-Appel
Designers
Claudia Fischer-Appel, Lars Nieb

0337
Art Director
Claudia Fischer-Appel
Designers
Claudia Fischer-Appel, Lars Nieb
Client
Ligalux GmbH
Tools/Software/Platform
Freehand
Paper/Materials
Munken & Luxomagi

0338
Art Director
Claudia Fischer-Appel
Designers
Claudia Fischer-Appel, Lars Nieb
Client
Ligalux GmbH
Tools/Software/Platform
Freehand
Paper/Materials
Munken & Luxomagi

0339
Art Director
Claudia Fischer-Appel
Designers
Claudia Fischer-Appel, Lars Nieb
Client
Ligalux GmbH
Tools/Software/Platform
Freehand
Paper/Materials
Munken & Luxomagi

0340/0366
Art Director
Claudia Fischer-Appel
Designers
Claudia Fischer-Appel, Lars Nieb
Client
Ligalux GmbH
Tools/Software/Platform
Freehand
Paper/Materials
Munken & Luxomagi

0679
Art Director
Petra Matouschek
Designer
Behruz Tschaitschian
Client
Augusta Technologie AG
Tools/Software/Platform
QuarkXPress, Freehand
Fonts
Bembo, Chalet Colgne

0680
Art Director
Martina Massong
Designer
Martina Massong
Client
Dentist's Practice Sattler and Jakel
Tools/Software/Platform
QuarkXPress
Fonts

Alternate Gothic, Bembo

0681
Art Director
Petra Matouschek
Designers
Christian Dworak, Meike Teubner
Client
Bundesknappschaft
Tools/Software/Platform
QuarkXPress, Freehand
Fonts
DTI Prokyon, Profile, Zurich

0682
Art Director
Petra Matouschek
Designers
Christian Dworak, Meike Teubner
Client
Bundesknappschaft
Tools/Software/Platform
QuarkXPress, Freehand

0697
Art Director
Petra Matouschek
Designer
Behruz Tschaitschian
Client
Augusta Technologie AG
Tools/Software/Platform
QuarkXPress, Freehand

0699
Art Director
Petra Matouschek
Designer
Behruz Tschaitschian
Client
Augusta Technologie AG
Tools/Software/Platform
QuarkXPress, Freehand

0699
Art Director
Petra Matouschek
Designer
Behruz Tschaitschian
Client
Augusta Technologie AG
Tools/Software/Platform
QuarkXPress, Freehand

0700
Art Director
Petra Matouschek
Designer
Behruz Tschaitschian
Client
Augusta Technologie AG
Tools/Software/Platform
QuarkXPress, Freehand

0702
Art Directors
Petra Matouschek, Martina Massong
Designers
Martina Massong, Vicky Abndt
Client

Client
Fischer Appelt Kommunikation, GmbH
Tools/Software/Platform
QuarkXPress, Freehand
Fonts
DTL Elzevire, Helvetica Neue

0703
Art Director
Hedda Gerdes
Designer
Sylvia Kossmann
Client
MSD Sharp & Dohme

Lippa Pearce Design, London

0202
Art Director
Harry Pearce
Client
Phaidon

0581
Art Director
Domenic Lippa
Designer
Domenic Lippa
Client
The Typographic Circle

0582
Art Director
Domenic Lippa
Designer
Domenic Lippa
Client
The Typographic Circle

0583
Art Director
Domenic Lippa
Designer
Domenic Lippa
Client
The Typographic Circle

0584
Art Director
Domenic Lippa
Designer
Domenic Lippa
Client
The Typographic Circle

0585
Art Director
Domenic Lippa
Designer
Domenic Lippa
Client
The Typographic Circle

0586
Art Director
Domenic Lippa
Designer
Domenic Lippa
Client
The Typographic Circle

0588
Art Director
Domenic Lippa
Designer
Domenic Lippa
Client

Pilot Light

0786
Art Director
Domenic Lippa
Designer
Domenic Lippa
Client
The Typographic Circle

0787
Art Director
Domenic Lippa
Designer
Domenic Lippa
Client
The Typographic Circle

0790
Art Director
Domenic Lippa
Designer
Domenic Lippa
Client
The Typographic Circle

0813
TK?

0850
Art Director
Harry Pearce
Designer
Harry Pearce
Client
Science Museum-Dana Centre

0901
Art Director
Harry Pearce
Designer
Harry Pearce
Client
Science Museum-Dana Centre

0893
Art Director
Harry Pearce
Designer
Harry Pearce
Client
Science Museum-Dana Centre

0904
Art Director
Domenic Lippa
Designer
Domenic Lippa
Client
Geronimo Inns

0916
Art Director
Harry Pearce
Designer
Harry Pearce
Client
Lippa Pearce

0949
Art Director
Domenic Lippa
Designer
Domenic Lippa
Client
Geronimo Inns

0970
Art Director
Harry Pearce
Designer
Harry Pearce
Client
Science Museum-

Dana Centre

Liska & Associates

0435
Art Director
Tanya Quick
Designer
Jonathan Seeds
Client
Luxi
Tools/Software/Platform
Adobe Illustrator
Font
Hand drawn

LSD

0008
Art Directors
Sonia Diaz, Gabriel Martinez
Designer
Gabriel Martinez
Client
LSDspace
Tools/Software/Platform
Freehand, Fontographer
Fonts
Arial Symbol, Avenir Utopia, Bembo Bomb 11M, Impacto, Optima Neo, Pepita Analfabeta, Rotis Sans Perfekt, Sans Futura, Times Sweet Times, Univers Corporation

0009
Art Directors
Sonia Diaz, Gabriel Martinez
Designer
Gabriel Martinez
Client
LSDspace
Tools/Software/Platform
Freehand, Fontographer
Fonts
Arial Symbol, Avenir Utopia, Bembo Bomb 11M, Impacto, Optima Neo, Pepita Analfabeta, Rotis Sans Perfekt, Sans Futura, Times Sweet Times, Univers Corporation

0014
Art Directors
Sonia Diaz, Gabriel Martinez
Designer
Gabriel Martinez
Client
LSDspace
Tools/Software/Platform
Freehand, Fontographer
Fonts
Arial Symbol, Avenir Utopia, Bembo Bomb 11M, Impacto, Optima Neo, Pepita Analfabeta, Rotis Sans Perfekt, Sans Futura, Times Sweet Times, Univers Corporation

0015
Art Directors
Sonia Diaz, Gabriel Martinez

Designer
Gabriel Martinez
Client
LSDspace
Tools/Software/Platform
Freehand, Fontographer
Fonts
Arial Symbol, Avenir Utopia, Bembo Bomb 11M, Impacto, Optima Neo, Pepita Analfabeta, Rotis Sans Perfekt, Sans Futura, Times Sweet Times, Univers Corporation

0016
Art Directors
Sonia Diaz, Gabriel Martinez
Designer
Gabriel Martinez
Client
LSDspace
Tools/Software/Platform
Freehand, Fontographer
Fonts
Arial Symbol, Avenir Utopia, Bembo Bomb 11M, Impacto, Optima Neo, Pepita Analfabeta, Rotis Sans Perfekt, Sans Futura, Times Sweet Times, Univers Corporation

0017
Art Directors
Sonia Diaz, Gabriel Martinez
Designer
Gabriel Martinez
Client
LSDspace
Tools/Software/Platform
Freehand, Fontographer
Fonts
Arial Symbol, Avenir Utopia, Bembo Bomb 11M, Impacto, Optima Neo, Pepita Analfabeta, Rotis Sans Perfekt, Sans Futura, Times Sweet Times, Univers Corporation

0023
Art Directors
Sonia Diaz, Gabriel Martinez
Designer
Gabriel Martinez
Client
LSDspace
Tools/Software/Platform
Freehand, Fontographer
Fonts
Arial Symbol, Avenir Utopia, Bembo Bomb 11M, Impacto, Optima Neo, Pepita Analfabeta, Rotis Sans Perfekt, Sans Futura, Times Sweet Times, Univers Corporation

0024
Art Directors
Sonia Diaz, Gabriel Martinez
Designer

Gabriel Martinez
Client
LSDspace
Tools/Software/Platform
Freehand, Fontographer
Fonts
Arial Symbol, Avenir Utopia, Bembo Bomb 11M, Impacto, Optima Neo, Pepita Analfabeta, Rotis Sans Perfekt, Sans Futura, Times Sweet Times, Univers Corporation

0025
Art Directors
Sonia Diaz, Gabriel Martinez
Designer
Gabriel Martinez
Client
LSDspace
Tools/Software/Platform
Freehand, Fontographer
Fonts
Arial Symbol, Avenir Utopia, Bembo Bomb 11M, Impacto, Optima Neo, Pepita Analfabeta, Rotis Sans Perfekt, Sans Futura, Times Sweet Times, Univers Corporation

0026
Art Directors
Sonia Diaz, Gabriel Martinez
Designer
Gabriel Martinez
Client
LSDspace
Tools/Software/Platform
Freehand, Fontographer
Fonts
Arial Symbol, Avenir Utopia, Bembo Bomb 11M, Impacto, Optima Neo, Pepita Analfabeta, Rotis Sans Perfekt, Sans Futura, Times Sweet Times, Univers Corporation

0027
Art Directors
Sonia Diaz, Gabriel Martinez
Designer
Gabriel Martinez
Client
LSDspace
Tools/Software/Platform
Freehand, Fontographer
Fonts
Arial Symbol, Avenir Utopia, Bembo Bomb 11M, Impacto, Optima Neo, Pepita Analfabeta, Rotis Sans Perfekt, Sans Futura, Times Sweet Times, Univers Corporation

0028
Art Directors
Sonia Diaz, Gabriel Martinez
Designer
Gabriel Martinez

Client
LSDspace
Tools/Software/Platform
Freehand, Fontographer
Fonts
Arial Symbol, Avenir Utopia, Bembo Bomb 11M, Impacto, Optima Neo, Pepita Analfabeta, Rotis Sans Perfekt, Sans Futura, Times Sweet Times, Univers Corporation

0029
Art Directors
Sonia Diaz, Gabriel Martinez
Designer
Gabriel Martinez
Client
LSDspace
Tools/Software/Platform
Freehand, Fontographer
Fonts
Arial Symbol, Avenir Utopia, Bembo Bomb 11M, Impacto, Optima Neo, Pepita Analfabeta, Rotis Sans Perfekt, Sans Futura, Times Sweet Times, Univers Corporation

0030
Art Directors
Sonia Diaz, Gabriel Martinez
Designer
Gabriel Martinez
Client
LSDspace
Tools/Software/Platform
Freehand, Fontographer
Fonts
Arial Symbol, Avenir Utopia, Bembo Bomb 11M, Impacto, Optima Neo, Pepita Analfabeta, Rotis Sans Perfekt, Sans Futura, Times Sweet Times, Univers Corporation

0031
Art Directors
Sonia Diaz, Gabriel Martinez
Designer
Gabriel Martinez
Client
LSDspace
Tools/Software/Platform
Freehand, Fontographer
Fonts
Arial Symbol, Avenir Utopia, Bembo Bomb 11M, Impacto, Optima Neo, Pepita Analfabeta, Rotis Sans Perfekt, Sans Futura, Times Sweet Times, Univers Corporation

0032
Art Directors
Sonia Diaz, Gabriel Martinez
Designer
Gabriel Martinez
Client
LSDspace

0061
Art Directors
Sonia Diaz, Gabriel Martinez
Designer
Gabriel Martinez
Client
LSDspace
Tools/Software/Platform
Freehand, Fontographer
Fonts
Arial Symbol, Avenir Utopia, Bembo Bomb 11M, Impacto, Optima Neo, Pepita Analfabeta, Rotis Sans Perfekt, Sans Futura, Times Sweet Times, Univers Corporation

0062
Art Directors
Sonia Diaz, Gabriel Martinez
Designer
Gabriel Martinez
Client
LSDspace
Tools/Software/Platform
Freehand, Fontographer
Fonts
Arial Symbol, Avenir Utopia, Bembo Bomb 11M, Impacto, Optima Neo, Pepita Analfabeta, Rotis Sans Perfekt, Sans Futura, Times Sweet Times, Univers Corporation

0063
Art Directors
Sonia Diaz, Gabriel Martinez
Designer
Gabriel Martinez
Client
LSDspace
Tools/Software/Platform
Freehand, Fontographer
Fonts
Arial Symbol, Avenir Utopia, Bembo Bomb 11M, Impacto, Optima Neo, Pepita Analfabeta, Rotis Sans Perfekt, Sans Futura, Times Sweet Times, Univers Corporation

0064
Art Directors
Sonia Diaz, Gabriel Martinez
Designer
Gabriel Martinez
Client
LSDspace

Tools/Software/Platform
Freehand, Fontographer
Fonts
Arial Symbol, Avenir Utopia, Bembo Bomb 11M, Impacto, Optima Neo, Pepita Analfabeta, Rotis Sans Perfekt, Sans Futura, Times Sweet Times, Univers Corporation

0065
Art Directors
Sonia Diaz, Gabriel Martinez
Designer
Gabriel Martinez
Client
LSDspace
Tools/Software/Platform
Freehand, Fontographer
Fonts
Arial Symbol, Avenir Utopia, Bembo Bomb 11M, Impacto, Optima Neo, Pepita Analfabeta, Rotis Sans Perfekt, Sans Futura, Times Sweet Times, Univers Corporation

0066
Art Directors
Sonia Diaz, Gabriel Martinez
Designer
Gabriel Martinez
Client
LSDspace
Tools/Software/Platform
Freehand, Fontographer
Fonts
Arial Symbol, Avenir Utopia, Bembo Bomb 11M, Impacto, Optima Neo, Pepita Analfabeta, Rotis Sans Perfekt, Sans Futura, Times Sweet Times, Univers Corporation

0079
Art Directors
Sonia Diaz, Gabriel Martinez
Designer
Gabriel Martinez
Client
LSDspace
Tools/Software/Platform
Freehand, Fontographer
Font
Bamboo Bold 11M, Pepita Analfabeta, Univers Corporation

0080
Art Directors
Sonia Diaz, Gabriel Martinez
Designer
Gabriel Martinez
Client
LSDspace
Tools/Software/Platform
Freehand, Fontographer
Fonts
Bamboo Bold 11M, Pepita Analfabeta, Univers Corporation

0081
Art Directors
Sonia Diaz, Gabriel Martinez
Designer
Gabriel Martinez
Client
LSDspace
Tools/Software/Platform
Freehand, Fontographer
Font
Bamboo Bold 11M, Pepita Analfabeta, Univers Corporation

0082
Art Directors
Sonia Diaz, Gabriel Martinez
Designer
Gabriel Martinez
Client
LSDspace
Tools/Software/Platform
Freehand, Fontographer
Font
Bamboo Bold 11M, Pepita Analfabeta, Univers Corporation

0105
Art Directors
Sonia Diaz, Gabriel Martinez
Designer
Gabriel Martinez
Client
LSDspace
Tools/Software/Platform
Freehand, Fontographer
Font
Avenir Utopia

0106
Art Directors
Sonia Diaz, Gabriel Martinez
Designer
Gabriel Martinez
Client
LSDspace
Tools/Software/Platform
Freehand, Fontographer
Font
Avenir Utopia

0107
Art Directors
Sonia Diaz, Gabriel Martinez
Designer
Gabriel Martinez
Client
LSDspace
Tools/Software/Platform
Freehand, Fontographer
Font
Avenir Utopia

0108
Art Directors
Sonia Diaz, Gabriel Martinez
Designer
Gabriel Martinez
Client
LSDspace
Tools/Software/Platform
Freehand, Fontographer
Font
Avenir Utopia

0109
Art Directors
Sonia Diaz, Gabriel Martinez
Designer
Gabriel Martinez
Client
LSDspace
Tools/Software/Platform
Freehand, Fontographer
Font
Avenir Utopia

0110
Art Directors
Sonia Diaz, Gabriel Martinez
Designer
Gabriel Martinez
Client
LSDspace
Tools/Software/Platform
Freehand, Fontographer
Font
Avenir Utopia

0117
Art Directors
Sonia Diaz, Gabriel Martinez
Designer
Gabriel Martinez
Client
LSDspace
Tools/Software/Platform
Freehand, Fontographer
Font
Times Sweet Times

0118
Art Directors
Sonia Diaz, Gabriel Martinez
Designer
Gabriel Martinez
Client
LSDspace
Tools/Software/Platform
Freehand, Fontographer
Font
Times Sweet Times

0119
Art Directors
Sonia Diaz, Gabriel Martinez
Designer
Gabriel Martinez
Client
LSDspace
Tools/Software/Platform
Freehand, Fontographer
Font
Times Sweet Times

0120
Art Directors
Sonia Diaz, Gabriel Martinez
Designer
Gabriel Martinez
Client
LSDspace
Tools/Software/Platform
Freehand, Fontographer
Font
Times Sweet Times

0121
Art Directors
Sonia Diaz, Gabriel Martinez
Designer
Gabriel Martinez

Font
Customized (all by
Lars Harmsen)

Marius Fahmer Design
0940
Art Director
Marius Fahmer
Designer
Marius Fahmer
Client
Reset Printery
Tools/Software/Platform
Freehand
Paper/Materials
Invercoat, 16epa
300g

Metal
0591
Art Director
Peat Jariya
Designer
Peat Jariya
Client
Reliance

0686
Art Director
Peat Jariya
Designer
Peat Jariya
Client
Reliance

0727
Art Director
Peat Jariya
Designer
Peat Jariya
Client
Reliance

Mike Salisbury, LLC
0813
Art Director
Mike Salisbury
Designer
Jill Bell
Client
South Coast Plaza
Tools/Software/Platform
Hand Lettered
Font
Hand drawn

Milton Glaser Inc.
0375
Art Director
Milton Glaser
Designer
Milton Glaser
Client
Double Nickel
Tools/Software/Platform
Adobe Illustrator
Font
Helvetica Rounded

Mires
0712
Art Director
Jose Serrano
Designer
Gale Spitzley
Client
J.F. Shea Company
Paper/Materials
Cover: Sundance
Felt, Inside: Gilbert
Relm

Miriello Grafico, Inc.
0003
Art Director
Dennis Garcia
Designer
Dennis Garcia
Client
Self-promo
Tools/Software/Platform
Adobe Illustrator,
Adobe Photoshop
Font
Trade Gothic

0019
Art Director
Dennis Garcia
Designer
Dennis Garcia
Client
Self-promo
Tools/Software/Platform
Adobe Illustrator,
Adobe Photoshop
Font
Trade Gothic

0021
Art Director
Dennis Garcia
Designer
Dennis Garcia
Client
Self-promotion
Tools/Software/Platform
Adobe Illustrator,
Adobe Photoshop
Font
Trade Gothic

0054
Art Director
Ron Miriello
Designer
Chris Keeney
Client
Fox River Paper
Tools/Software/Platform
Adobe Illustrator,
Adobe Photoshop
Paper/Materials
Starwhite Vicksburg

0055
Art Director
Ron Miriello
Designer
Chris Keeney
Client
Fox River Paper
Tools/Software/Platform
Adobe Illustrator,
Adobe Photoshop
Paper/Materials
Starwhite Vicksburg

0056
Art Director
Ron Miriello
Designer
Chris Keeney
Client
Fox River Paper
Tools/Software/Platform
Adobe Illustrator,
Adobe Photoshop
Paper/Materials
Starwhite Vicksburg

0057
Art Director
Ron Miriello
Designer
Chris Keeney
Client
Fox River Paper
Tools/Software/Platform
Adobe Illustrator,

Adobe Photoshop
Paper/Materials
Starwhite Vicksburg
0087
Art Director
Dennis Garcia
Designer
Dennis Garcia
Client
Self-promotion
Tools/Software/Platform
Adobe Illustrator,
Adobe Photoshop
Font
Trade Gothic

0092
Art Director
Dennis Garcia
Designer
Dennis Garcia
Client
Self-promo
Tools/Software/Platform
Adobe Illustrator,
Adobe Photoshop
Font
Trade Gothic

0146
Art Director
Dennis Garcia
Designer
Dennis Garcia
Client
Self-promotion
Tools/Software/Platform
Adobe Illustrator,
Adobe Photoshop
Font
Trade Gothic

0170
Art Director
Dennis Garcia
Designer
Dennis Garcia
Client
Self-promotion
Tools/Software/Platform
Adobe Illustrator,
Adobe Photoshop
Font
Trade Gothic

Mirko Ilii Corp.
0251
Art Director
Mirko Ilii
Designer
Mirko Ilii
Client
SLM
Tools/Software/Platform
QuarkXPress
Font
Interstate

0297
Art Director
Mirko Ilii
Designer
Mirko Ilii
Client
SLM
Tools/Software/Platform
QuarkXPress
Font
Interstate

Mixer
0762
Art Director
Erich Brechbuhl
Designer
Erich Brechbuhl
Client
Kulturkeller (im

Schtei), Sempach
Tools/Software/Platform
Freehand
0760
Art Director
Erich Brechbuhl
Designer
Erich Brechbuhl
Client
Kulturkeller (im
Schtei), Sempach
Tools/Software/Platform
Freehand

Modern Dog
0758
Art Director
Michael Strassburger
Designer
Michael Strassburger
Client
House of Blues
Tools/Software/Platform
Adobe Illustrator,
Adobe Photoshop,
Adobe InDesign
Font
Customized

0853
Art Director
Junichi Tsuneoka
Designer
Junichi Tsuneoka
Client
House of Blues
Tools/Software/Platform
Adobe Illustrator,
Adobe Photoshop,
Adobe InDesign
Font
Customized

0863
Art Director
Robynne Raye
Designer
Robynne Raye
Client
House of Blues
Tools/Software/Platform
Adobe Illustrator,
Adobe Photoshop,
Adobe InDesign
Font
Customized

0864
Art Director
Robynne Raye
Designer
Robynne Raye
Client
House of Blues
Tools/Software/Platform
Adobe Illustrator,
Adobe InDesign
Font
Customized

0866
Art Director
Robynne Raye
Designer
Robynne Raye
Client
House of Blues
Tools/Software/Platform
Adobe Illustrator,
Adobe Photoshop,
Adobe InDesign
Font
Customized

0867
Art Director
Michael Strassburger

Designer
Michael Strassburger
Client
House of Blues
Tools/Software/Platform
Adobe Illustrator,
Adobe Photoshop,
Adobe InDesign
Font
Customized

Monster Design
0640
Art Directors
Hannah Wygal,
Theresa Monica
Designers
Madeleine Eiche,
Denise Sakaki
Client
The Press
Tools/Software/Platform
Adobe Photoshop,
Freehand
Font
Garamond, Avenir,
French Script,
Bodoni, Carta,
Courier, Futura,
Helvetica, Hoefler,
Misproject, Postino,
Print Error, Sho,
Times, Trixie,
Univers, VAG

Motive Design Research
0521
Art Directors
Michael Connors,
Kari Strand
Designer
Peter Anderson
Client
Motive Design
Research
Tools/Software/Platform
QuarkXPress, Adobe
Photoshop
Paper/Materials
French Construction,
Classic Crest Label,
Glassing Bag,
Wildflower Seeds

0657
Art Directors
Michael Connors,
Kari Strand
Designer
Peter Anderson
Client
Motive Design
Research
Tools/Software/Platform
QuarkXPress, Adobe
Photoshop
Paper/Materials
French Construction,
Classic Crest Label,
Glassing Bag,
Wildflower Seeds

0671
Art Directors
Michael Connors,
Kari Strand
Designer
Kris Delaney
Client
Getty Images
Tools/Software/Platform
QuarkXPress,
Freehand, Adobe
Photoshop
Paper/Materials

Designer
Michael Strassburger
Client
House of Blues
Tools/Software/Platform
Adobe Illustrator,
Adobe Photoshop,
Adobe InDesign
Font
Customized

Starwhite Vicksburg,
Chl clear
0944
Art Directors
Michael Connors,
Kari Strand
Designer
Kris Delaney
Client
Getty Images
Tools/Software/Platform
QuarkXPress,
Freehand, Adobe
Photoshop
Paper/Materials
Starwhite Vicksburg,
Chl clear

Muggie Ramadani Design Studio
0410
Art Director
Muggie Ramadani
Designer
Muggie Ramadani
Client
Mikkel Bache,
Photographer
Tools/Software/Platform
Adobe Photoshop,
Adobe Illustrator
Font
Din

0438
Art Director
Muggie Ramadani
Designer
Muggie Ramadani
Client
Rebel Hairdesign
Tools/Software/Platform
Adobe Photoshop,
Adobe Illustrator,
QuarkXPress
Font
Helvetica Neue,
customized

0466
Art Director
Muggie Ramadani
Designer
Muggie Ramadani
Client
Mikkel Bache,
Photographer
Tools/Software/Platform
Adobe Photoshop,
Adobe Illustrator

0467
Art Director
Muggie Ramadani
Designer
Muggie Ramadani
Client
Peter Krasilnikoff,
Photographer
Tools/Software/Platform
Adobe Photoshop,
Adobe Illustrator
Font
Helvetica Neue,
customized

0468
Art Director
Muggie Ramadani
Designer
Muggie Ramadani
Client
Mikkel Bache,
Photographer
Tools/Software/Platform
Adobe Photoshop,

Adobe Illustrator
0481
Art Director
Muggie Ramadani
Designer
Muggie Ramadani
Client
Peter Krasilnikoff,
Photographer
Tools/Software/Platform
Adobe Photoshop,
Adobe Illustrator

0617
Art Director
Muggie Ramadani
Designer
Muggie Ramadani
Client
Port à Gauche
Tools/Software/Platform
Adobe Photoshop,
Adobe Illustrator
Fonts
Helvetica Neue,
designed font (logo)

0620
Art Director
Muggie Ramadani
Designer
Muggie Ramadani
Client
Peter Krasilnikoff,
Photographer
Tools/Software/Platform
Adobe Photoshop,
Adobe Illustrator
Fonts
Helvetica Neue,
designed font (logo)

0625
Art Director
Muggie Ramadani
Designer
Muggie Ramadani
Client
Peter Krasilnikoff,
Photographer
Tools/Software/Platform
Adobe Photoshop,
Adobe Illustrator
Fonts
Helvetica Neue,
designed font (logo)

0899
Art Director
Muggie Ramadani
Designer
Muggie Ramadani
Client
Dansk Basketball
Forbund
Tools/Software/Platform
Adobe Photoshop,
Adobe Illustrator
Font
Beta Sans

0939
Art Director
Muggie Ramadani
Designer
Muggie Ramadani
Client
Rebel Hairdesign
Tools/Software/Platform
Adobe Photoshop,
Adobe Illustrator,
QuarkXPress
Fonts
Helvetica Neue,
customized (logo)

NB: Studio
0348

Art Director
Alan Dye, Ben Stott,
Nich Finney
Designer
Jodie Wightman
Client
The Hub
Tools/Software/Platform
QuarkXPress, Adobe
Illustrator
Paper/Materials
Mffd custom hote
Font
Century Gothic,
Schnefeter

0477
Art Director
Alan Dye, Ben Stott,
Nich Finney
Designer
Nich Vincent
Client
The Hub/Centre for
Craft and Design
Tools/Software/Platform
QuarkXPress, Adobe
Illustrator
Fonts
Century Gothic,
Schnefeter

0564
Art Director
Alan Dye, Nich
Finney, Ben Stott
Designer
Nich Vincent
Client
The RSA
Tools/Software/Platform
Adobe Illustrator,
QuarkXPress
Font
Akzidenz Grotesk

0675
Art Director
Alan Dye, Nich
Finney, Ben Stott
Designer
Nich Vincent, Charlie
Smith
Client
Merchant
Tools/Software/Platform
Paper/ Materials
7xstocks from
Fenner Paper

0673
Art Director
Alan Dye, Nich
Finney, Ben Stott
Designer
Nich Vincent, Charlie
Smith
Client
Merchant
Paper/ Materials
7xstocks from
Fenner Paper

0677
Art Director
Alan Dye, Nich
Finney, Ben Stott
Designer
Nich Vincent, Charlie
Smith
Client
Merchant
Paper/ Materials
7xstocks from
Fenner Paper

0766
Art Director

Alan Dye, Nich
Finney, Ben Stott
Designer
Nich Vincent
Client
Tate Britain – Art of
the Garden
Tools/Software/Platform
QuarkXPress, Adobe
Illustrator
Font
Tate Bold

0800
Art Director
Alan Dye, Nich
Finney, Ben Stott
Designer
I. Pierce
Client
Jerwood – Crafts
Council
Tools/Software/Platform
QuarkXPress, Adobe
Photoshop
Font
AG Buch Stencil

0851
Art Director
Alan Dye, Nich
Finney, Ben Stott
Designer
Ben Stott
Client
Polygram Films
Tools/Software/Platform
QuarkXPress, Adobe
Photoshop

0910
Art Director
Alan Dye, Nich
Finney, Ben Stott
Designer
Alan Dye
Client
NIN Comscvp
Tools/Software/Platform
QuarkXPress
Font
Trajan

0931
Art Director
Alan Dye, Nich
Finney, Ben Stott
Designer
Nich Vincent
Client
D & AD
Tools/Software/Platform
QuarkXPress, Adobe
Illustrator
Font
Franklin Gothic

Niklaus
Troxler Design
0792
Art Director
Niklaus Troxler
Designer
Niklaus Troxler
Client
APG, Luzern
Tools/Software/Platform
QuarkXPress

0793
Art Director
Niklaus Troxler
Designer
Niklaus Troxler
Client
Jazz in Willisau
Paper/Materials
Handmade, brush
FontographerHand

drawn
0794
Art Director
Niklaus Troxler
Designer
Niklaus Troxler
Client
Jazz in Willisau
Paper/Materials
Handmade, stamp
letters

0795
Art Director
Niklaus Troxler
Designer
Niklaus Troxler
Client
Rathaus Willisan
Tools/Software/Platform
Adobe Illustrator
Font
Helvetica

Non-Format
0132
Art Directors
Kjell Ekmorn,
Kjell Ekmorn,
Jon Forss
Client
B3 Media
Font
Avant Garde,
customized

0281
Art Directors
Kjell Ekmorn,
Jon Forss
Designers
Kjell Ekmorn,
Jon Forss
Client
The Leaf Label
Font
FontographerFutura,
customized

0282
Art Directors
Kjell Ekmorn,
Jon Forss
Designers
Kjell Ekmorn,
Jon Forss
Client
Accidental Records
Font
Bookman

Origin
0783
Designer
Mark Bottomley
Client
Wigan Jazz Festival
Font
Woodblock

0784
Designer
Mark Bottomley
Client
Wigan Jazz Festival
Font
Woodblock

P22
0172
Art Director
Richard Kegler
Designers
Colin Kahn, R. Kegler
Client
P22 Type Foundry
Tools/Software/Platform
Adobe Illustrator,
Freehand/Mac
Font

Client
The Leaf Label
Font
Futura, customized

0354
Art Directors
Kjell Ekmorn,
Jon Forss
Designers
Kjell Ekmorn,
Jon Forss
Client
The Leaf Label
Font
Futura, customized

0355
Art Directors
Kjell Ekmorn,
Jon Forss
Designers
Kjell Ekmorn,
Jon Forss
Client
The Leaf Label
Font
Futura, customized

0356
Art Directors
Kjell Ekmorn,
Jon Forss
Designers
Kjell Ekmorn,
Jon Forss
Client
The Wire Magazine

0357
Art Directors
Kjell Ekmorn,
Jon Forss
Designers
Kjell Ekmorn,
Jon Forss
Client
The Wire Magazine

0973
Art Directors
Kjell Ekmorn,
Jon Forss
Designers
Kjell Ekmorn,
Jon Forss
Client

0283
Art Directors
Kjell Ekmorn,
Jon Forss
Designers
Kjell Ekmorn,
Jon Forss
Client
The Wire Magazine

0288
Art Directors
Kjell Ekmorn,
Jon Forss
Designers
Kjell Ekmorn,
Jon Forss
Client
The Wire Magazine

0343
Art Directors
Kjell Ekmorn,
Jon Forss
Designers
Kjell Ekmorn,
Jon Forss

Ed Rogers font set

0173
Art Director
Richard Kegler
Designers
Colin Kahn, R. Kegler
Client
P22 Type Foundry
Tools/Software/Platform
Adobe Illustrator,
Freehand/Mac
Font
Bagaglio font set

0174
Art Director
Richard Kegler
Designers
Colin Kahn, R. Kegler
Client
P22 Type Foundry
Tools/Software/Platform
Adobe Illustrator,
Freehand/Mac
Font
London Underground
font set

0175
Art Director
Richard Kegler
Designers
Colin Kahn, R. Kegler
Client
P22 Type Foundry
Tools/Software/Platform
Adobe Illustrator,
Freehand/Mac
Font
Pop Art font set

0176
Art Director
Richard Kegler
Designers
Colin Kahn, R. Kegler
Client
P22 Type Foundry
Tools/Software/Platform
Adobe Illustrator,
Freehand/Mac
Font
Dada

Pangaro Beer
0614
Art Directors
Natalie Pangaro,
Shannon Beer
Designer
David Salfia
Client
Harvard Medical
School
Tools/Software/Platform
QuarkXPress
Fonts
Rotis, Interstate

Paul Shaw/
Letter Design
0139
Art Director
Paul Shaw
Designer
Paul Shaw
Client
Paul Shaw/Letter
Design & Peter Kruty
Editions
Tools/Software/Platform
QuarkXPress,
Letterpress
Font
Futura

Ph.D

0372
Art Directors
Clive Piercy, Michael
Hodgson
Designers
Clive Piercy, Carol
Kono-Noble, Tammy
Dotson
Client
Foundation Press
Tools/Software/Platform
QuarkXPress

0374
Art Directors
Clive Piercy, Michael
Hodgson
Designers
Clive Piercy, Carol
Kond-Noble, Tammy
Dotson
Client
Foundation Press
Tools/Software/Platform
QuarkXPress

0376
Art Directors
Clive Piercy, Michael
Hodgson
Designers
Carol Kond-Noble,
Clive Piercy
Client
Quicksilver Edition
Tools/Software/Platform
QuarkXPress
Font
Trade Gothic

0423
Art Directors
Clive Piercy, Michael
Hodgson
Designers
Carol Kond-Noble,
Clive Piercy
Client
Quicksilver Edition
Tools/Software/Platform
QuarkXPress
Font
Trade Gothic

0472
Art Directors
Clive Piercy, Michael
Hodgson
Designer
Tammy Dotson
Client
Cloutier Agency
Tools/Software/Platform
Adobe Illustrator
Fonts
Bauer Bodoni, Adine
Kimberg, Ironmonger

0478
Art Directors
Clive Piercy, Michael
Hodgson
Designers
Michael Hodgson
Client
Primary Color
Tools/Software/Platform
QuarkXPress
Font
Trade Gothic,
Interstate

Phyx Design
0606
Art Director
Masaki Koike
Designer
Masaki Koike
Tools/Software/Platform

Screen Print, Hands
Paper/Materials
French Paper
Company –
Construction

Piscatello
Design Centre
0785
Art Director
Rocco Piscatello
Designer
Rocco Piscatello
Client
Fashion Institute of
Technology
Tools/Software/Platform
QuarkXPress
Font
Univers

Plan-B Studio
0256
Art Director
Luke Herriott
(Rotovision)
Designer
Steve Price
Client
Rotovision
Publishing
Tools/Software/Platform
Adobe Photoshop,
QuarkXPress
Paper/Materials
Black and White
darkroom, scalpels,
masking tape, ace-
tate, photocopier

0265
Art Director
Luke Herriott
(Rotovision)
Designer
Steve Price
Client
Rotovision
Publishing
Tools/Software/Platform
Adobe Photoshop,
QuarkXPress
Paper/Materials
Black and White
darkroom, scalpels,
masking tape, ace-
tate, photocopier

0284
Art Director
Luke Herriott
(Rotovision)
Designer
Steve Price
Client
Rotovision
Publishing
Tools/Software/Platform
Adobe Photoshop,
QuarkXPress
Paper/Materials
Black and White
darkroom, scalpels,
masking tape, ace-
tate, photocopier

0285
Art Director
Luke Herriott
(Rotovision)
Designer
Steve Price
Client
Rotovision
Publishing
Tools/Software/Platform
Adobe Photoshop,
QuarkXPress

Paper/Materials
Black and White
darkroom, scalpels,
masking tape, ace-
tate, photocopier

0296
Art Director
Nathan Gale
(Creative Review)
Designer
Steve Price
Client
Creative Review
Magazine, Centaur
Publications
Tools/Software/Platform
Adobe Illustrator,
Adobe Photos

0301
Art Director
Nathan Gale
(Creative Review)
Designer
Steve Price
Client
Creative Review
Magazine, Centaur
Publications
Tools/Software/Platform
Adobe Illustrator,
Adobe Photos

0937
Art Director
Steve Price
Client
Wall of Sound
Recordings
Tools/Software/Platform
Adobe Photoshop,
QuarkXPress

0974
Art Director
Steve Price
Client
Wall of Sound
Recordings
Tools/Software/Platform
Adobe Photoshop,
QuarkXPress

Planet 10
0416
Art Directors
Mike and Jennifer
Tuttle
Designer
Mike Tuttle
Client
Tony Stewart
Tools/Software/Platform
Freehand, Adobe
Photoshop
Font
Customized

Planet 10, Red Nose Studio
0499
Art Directors
Mike and Jennifer
Tuttle, Chris Sickels
Designers
Mike and Jennifer
Tuttle, Chris Sickels
Client
Quality Printing
Tools/Software/Platform
QuarkXPress, Adobe
Illustrator, Adobe
Photoshop

0500
Art Directors
Mike and Jennifer

Tuttle, Chris Sickels
Designer
Mike and Jennifer
Tuttle, Chris Sickels
Client
Quality Printing
Tools/Software/Platform
QuarkXPress, Adobe
Illustrator, Adobe
Photoshop

Playground Creative
No longer in business
0749
Art Director
Tim Bridle
Designer
Tim Bridle
Client
Wea/London
Tools/Software/Platform
Adobe Illustrator,
Adobe Photoshop,
QuarkXPress, photo-
copier, various
Font
Rosewood

Plus Gestaltung
0123
Art Director
Alexander Kranz
Designer
Alexander Kranz
Client
Self Promotion
Tools/Software/Platform
QuarkXPress

Point Blank
0128
Art Director
Point Blank
Designer
Point Blank
Client
MTV
Tools/Software/Platform
Adobe Photoshop,
Quark
Font
Customized

Polite Design Inc.
0764
Designers
Kerry Polite
Client
American Institute of
Architects
Tools/Software/Platform
Adobe Illustrator
Fonts
Frutiger

Q
0048
Art Director
Thilo Von Debschitz
Designers
Tanja Mann, David
Bascom
Client
Arjo Wiggins
Germany
Tools/Software/Platform
Freehand
Paper/Materials
Yearling Classic/
Jazz

0424

Art Director
Marcel Krummerer
Designer
Marcel Krummerer
Client
Wernoto
Tools/Software/Platform
Freehand
Font
Hand drawn

0476
Art Director
Lansert Nielbock
Designer
Marcel Krummerer
Client
M-real Zanders
Tools/Software/Platform
Freehand
Font
VAG Rounded

0491
Art Director
Marcel Krummerer
Designer
Marcel Krummerer
Client
Dreamshirt
Tools/Software/Platform
Freehand
Font
Mak 10

0730
Art Director
Thilo Von Debschitz
Designer
Karsten Muller
Client
Association of Plastic
Manufacturers
Tools/Software/Platform
Adobe Illustrator
Font
Alph Headline

R&MAG Graphic Design
0388
Art Director
Fontanella,
DiSomma, Cesar
Designer
Fontanella,
DiSomma, Cesar
Client
TRE servizi aziendali
integrati/Naples
Tools/Software/Platform
Adobe Illustrator
Fonts
Futura, Helvetica

0427
Art Director
Fontanella,
DiSomma, Cesar
Designer
Fontanella,
DiSomma, Cesar
Client
De Caro Expert/
Salerno
Tools/Software/Platform
Adobe Illustrator
Font
Franklin Gothic

0763
Art Director
Fontanella,
DiSomma, Cesar
Designer
Fontanella,
DiSomma, Cesar
Client

Rapprochment/
SNCF/Paris
Tools/Software/
Platform
Adobe Illustrator
Font
Helvetica

Rinzen
0480
Client
Family (Club)
Tools/Software/
Platform
Freehand
Paper/Materials
2 PMS, diecut and
spot UV, celloglase
Font
VAG Rounded

Rome & Gold Creative
0141
Art Director
Robert E. Goldie
Designers
Lorenzo Romero,
Zeke Sikelianos
Client
Rome & Gold
Creative
Tools/Software/
Platform
Adobe Illustrator
Font
Algerian

0421
Art Director
Robert E. Goldie
Designers
Lorenzo Romero,
Zeke Sikelianos
Client
New Mexico Ad
Federation
Tools/Software/
Platform
Adobe Illustrator
Font
Futura Medium

Rose Design
0413
Art Director
Simon Elliott
Designer
Esther Kirkpatrick
Client
AMP
Tools/Software/
Platform
Adobe Illustrator
Font
Hand drawn

0580
Art Director
Simon Elliott
Designer
Simon Elliott
Client
Royal Mail
Tools/Software/
Platform
QuarkXPress, Adobe
Illustrator, Adobe
Photoshop
Font
Base 9

0602
Art Director
Simon Elliott
Designer

Simon Elliott
Client
Westzone Publishing
Tools/Software/Platform
QuarkXPress, Adobe
Illustrator, Adobe
Photoshop
Paper/Materials
250 Cyclus, 120
(French Leaves)
Hello silk

0603
Art Director
Simon Elliott
Designer
Simon Elliott
Client
Westzone Publishing
Tools/Software/Platform
QuarkXPress, Adobe
Illustrator, Adobe
Photoshop
Paper/Materials
250 Cyclus, 120
(French Leaves)
Hello silk

0604
Art Director
Simon Elliott
Designer
Simon Elliott
Client
Westzone Publishing
Tools/Software/Platform
QuarkXPress, Adobe
Illustrator, Adobe
Photoshop
Paper/Materials
250 Cyclus, 120
(French Leaves)
Hello silk

0822
Art Director
Simon Elliott
Designer
Simon Elliott
Client
Tate Britain
Tools/Software/Platform
QuarkXPress, Adobe
Illustrator, Adobe
Photoshop
Font
Cooper Black Tate

Ryan Burlinson
0440
Art Director
Ryan Burlinson
Designer
Ryan Burlinson
Client
Suzie Capozza
Tools/Software/Platform
Adobe Illustrator
Font
Eurostile Bold
(customized)

Medhi Saeedi
0807
Art Director
Medhi Saeedi
Designer
Medhi Saeedi
Sepah Pasdaran
Tools/Software/Platform
Adobe Photoshop

0810
Art Director
Medhi Saeedi
Designer
Medhi Saeedi

Client
TV Basieeg
Tools/Software/Platform
Adobe Photoshop

0857
Art Director
Medhi Saeedi
Designer
Medhi Saeedi
Client
Iranian Graphic
Designer Society
(IGDS)
Tools/Software/Platform
Adobe Photoshop

Sagmeister Inc.
0799
Art Director
Stefan Sagmeister
Designers
Matthias
Ernstberger, Stefan
Sagmeister
Client
Art Grandeer Nature
Tools/Software/Platform
Adobe Photoshop
Font
Hand drawn

0806
Art Director
Stefan Sagmeister
Designers
Matthias
Ernstberger, Stefan
Sagmeister
Client
Art Grandeer Nature
Tools/Software/Platform
Adobe Photoshop
Font
Hand drawn

0847
Art Director
Stefan Sagmeister
Designers
Sagmeister Inc., Bela
Borsodi
Client
Copy
Magazine(Austria)
Tools/Software/Platform
Adobe Photoshop
Font
Hand drawn

SalterBaxter
0656
Art Director
Penny Baxter
Designer
Alan Delgado
Client
Salterbaxter &
Context
Tools/Software/Platform
QuarkXPress, Adobe
Illustrator
Paper/Materials
Flockage

Samen Weekende Ontwerpers
0449
Art Director
Andre Toet Scossa
Nostra)
Designer
François Gervais
Client
Best of Class Wines

SAS
0877
Art Director
Gilmar Wendt
Designer
John-Paul Sykes
Client
SAS
Tools/Software/Platform
Adobe Illustrator
Font
Baskerville

Scorsone/Drueding
0819
Art Directors
Joe Scorsone,
Alice Drueding
Designer
Joe Scorsone,
Alice Drueding
Client
Scorsone/Drueding
Tools/Software/Platform
Adobe Photoshop,
Adobe Illustrator
Fonts
Ironwood, Futura
Bold, hand drawn

Si Scott
0387
Art Director
Si Scott
Designer
Si Scott
Client
Endgunn
Tools/Software/Platform
Adobe Illustrator
Font
Futura

0417
Art Director
Si Scott
Designer
Si Scott
Client
Personal Project
Paper/Materials
Pens (black Felt)

0462
Art Director
Si Scott
Designer
Si Scott
Client
Personal Project
Tools/Software/Platform
QuarkXPress
Paper/Materials
Pens (black Felt)

Segura Inc.
0166
Art Director
Carlos Segura

0184
Art Director
Carlos Segura

0193
Art Director
Carlos Segura

0201
Art Director
Carlos Segura

0234
Art Director
Carlos Segura

0349
Art Director
Carlos Segura

0389
Art Director
Carlos Segura

0405
Art Director
Carlos Segura

0415
Art Director
Carlos Segura

0430
Art Director
Carlos Segura

0631
Art Director
Carlos Segura

0641
Art Director
Carlos Segura

0759
Art Director
Carlos Segura

0768
Art Director
Carlos Segura

0802
Art Director
Carlos Segura

0804
Art Director
Carlos Segura

0816
Art Director
Carlos Segura

0855
Art Director
Carlos Segura

0871
Art Director
Carlos Segura

0883
Art Director
Carlos Segura

0884
Art Director
Carlos Segura

0886
Art Director
Carlos Segura

0923
Art Director
Carlos Segura

0925
Art Director
Carlos Segura

0928
Art Director
Carlos Segura

0964
Art Director
Carlos Segura

0978
Art Director
Carlos Segura

Seltzer Design

0179
Art Director
Rochelle Seltzer
Designer
Meaghan O'Keefe
Client
Seltzer Design
Tools/Software/Platform
Adobe Illustrator CS
Fonts
Vivanti, Eldetic,
MBell, Lymphatic,
Dalliance, Futura
Condensed,
Garamond

0180
Art Director
Rochelle Seltzer
Designer
Meaghan O'Keefe
Client
Seltzer Design
Tools/Software/Platform
Adobe Illustrator CS
Fonts
Vivanti, Eldetic,
MBell, Lymphatic,
Dalliance, Futura
Condensed,
Garamond

0181
Art Director
Rochelle Seltzer
Designer
Meaghan O'Keefe
Client
Seltzer Design
Tools/Software/Platform
Adobe Illustrator CS
Fonts
Vivanti, Eldetic,
MBell, Lymphatic,
Dalliance, Futura
Condensed,
Garamond

0182
Art Director
Rochelle Seltzer
Designer
Meaghan O'Keefe
Client
Seltzer Design
Tools/Software/Platform
Adobe Illustrator CS
Fonts
Vivanti, Eldetic,
MBell, Lymphatic,
Dalliance, Futura
Condensed,
Garamond

Simon & Goetz Design

0402
Art Director
Bernd Vollmoller
Designer
Bernd Vollmoller
Client
Britta Janas, graphic
design production
Tools/Software/Platform
Freehand
Fonts
Candice, Bauer
Bodoni, Adobe
Garamond, Futura,
Centennial, Akzidenz
Grotesk

0469
Art Director
Bernd Vollmoller
Designer

Bernd Vollmoller
Client
Britta Janas, graphic
design production
Tools/Software/Platform
Freehand
Fonts
Candice, Bauer
Bodoni, Adobe
Garamond, Futura,
Centennial, Akzidenz
Grotesk

0513
Art Director
Thomas Wenzel
Designer
Thomas Wenzel
Client
ADP Engineering/
Rotwild
Tools/Software/Platform
Freehand

0514
Art Director
Thomas Wenzel
Designer
Thomas Wenzel
Client
ADP Engineering/
Rotwild
Tools/Software/Platform
Freehand

0516
Art Director
Thomas Wenzel
Designer
Thomas Wenzel
Client
ADP Engineering/
Rotwild
Tools/Software/Platform
Freehand

0517
Art Director
Volker Weinmann
Designer
Volker Weinmann
Client
ADP Engineering/
Rotwild
Tools/Software/Platform
Freehand
Font
Trade Gothic

0610
Art Director
Anne Mulder
Designer
Anne Mulder
Client
Open Air Systems
GmbH
Tools/Software/Platform
QuarkXPress
Fonts
Centennial, Din

Sommese Design

0672
Art Director
Lanny Sommese
Designers
Clinton Van Gemert,
Joe Shumbat, Roman
Shuman
Client
Penn State School of
Visual Arts
Tools/Software/Platform
Adobe Photoshop,
QuarkXPress

0725

Art Director
Kristin Breslin
Sommese
Designers
Alexis Camdanis,
Keith Cummings
Client
Penn State
Tools/Software/Platform
Adobe Photoshop,
Adobe Illustrator

0723
Art Director
Kristin Breslin
Sommese
Designers
Alexis Camdanis,
Keith Cummings
Client
Penn State
Tools/Software/Platform
Adobe Photoshop,
Adobe Illustrator

Smith Design

0913
Art Director
Laura Markley
Designer
Laura Markley
Client
Snapple Beverage
Group
Tools/Software/Platform
Adobe Photoshop,
Adobe Illustrator
Fonts
Kinison, Cosmos
(copy), hand drawn
(logo)

Jason Smith

0948
Art Director
Jason Smith
Designer
Jason Smith
Client
Self Promotion
Tools/Software/Platform
Adobe Illustrator,
Adobe Photoshop
Fonts
Customized

Starshot

0187
Art Director
Lars Harmsen
Designer
Lars Harmsen
Client
Starshot Byke Style
Magazine
Tools/Software/Platform
QXD, PSD, FH
Paper/Materials
Reflecting image by
Vogt-Druck

0247
Art Director
Lars Harmsen
Designer
Lars Harmsen
Client
Starshot Byke Style
Magazine
Tools/Software/Platform
QXD, PSD, FH
Paper/Materials
Reflecting image by
Vogt-Druck

0277
Art Director
Lars Harmsen

Designer
Lars Harmsen
Client
Starshot Byke Style
Magazine
Tools/Software/Platform
QXD, PSD, FH

0299
Art Director
Lars Harmsen
Designer
Lars Harmsen
Client
Starshot Byke Style
Magazine
Tools/Software/Platform
QXD, PSD, FH
Paper/Materials
Reflecting image by
Vogt-Druck

0300
Art Director
Lars Harmsen
Designer
Lars Harmsen
Client
Starshot Byke Style
Magazine
Tools/Software/Platform
QXD, PSD, FH
Paper/Materials
Reflecting image by
Vogt-Druck

0428
Art Director
Lars Harmsen
Designers
Lars Harmsen, Tina
Weisser, Claudia
Klein
Client
Starshot Byke Style
Magazine
Tools/Software/Platform
QXD, PSD, FH
Paper/Materials
Cover: Gmunder
Buttenpapier;
Collection Treasury,
Colour Value

0670
Art Director
Lars Harmsen
Designers
Lars Harmsen, Tina
Weisser, Claudia
Klein
Client
Starshot Byke Style
Magazine
Tools/Software/Platform
QXD, PSD, FH
Paper/Materials
Cover: Grund,
Buttenpapier,
Collection Vibe,
Colour Gentle Rose

0715
Art Director
Lars Harmsen
Designers
Lars Harmsen, Tina
Weisser, Claudia
Klein
Client
Starshot Byke Style
Magazine
Tools/Software/Platform
QXD, PSD, FH
Paper/Materials
Cover: Gmunder
Buttenpapier;

Designer
Lars Harmsen
Client
Starshot Byke Style
Magazine
Tools/Software/Platform
QXD, PSD, FH
Paper/Materials
Reflecting image by
Vogt-Druck

Collection Treasury,
Colour Value

0716
Art Director
Lars Harmsen
Designers
Lars Harmsen, Tina
Weisser, Claudia
Klein
Client
Starshot Byke Style
Magazine
Tools/Software/Platform
QXD, PSD, FH
Paper/Materials
Cover: Gmunder
Buttenpapier;
Collection Treasury,
Colour Value

0743
Art Director
Lars Harmsen
Designers
Lars Harmsen, Tina
Weisser
Client
Starshot Byke Style
Magazine
Tools/Software/Platform
QXD, PSD, FH
Paper/Materials
Cover: Grund,
Buttenpapier,
Collection Vibe,
Colour Gentle Rose

0745
Art Director
Lars Harmsen
Designers
Lars Harmsen, Tina
Weisser
Client
Starshot Byke Style
Magazine
Tools/Software/Platform
QXD, PSD, FH
Paper/Materials
Cover: Grund,
Buttenpapier,
Collection Vibe,
Colour Gentle Rose

Stoecker Design

0422
Art Director
James Stoecker
Designer
James Stoecker
Client
Nancy Hirstein
writer/editor
Tools/Software/Platform
Adobe Illustrator
Font
Akzidenz Grotesk

Strichpunkt

0038
Art Director
Kirsten Dietz
Designer
Kirsten Dietz
Client
Verlag Hermann
Schmidt Maint
Tools/Software/Platform
QuarkXPress/
Mac OS
Font
FF Scala

0041
Art Director
Kirsten Dietz

Designer
Kirsten Dietz
Client
Verlag Hermann
Schmidt Maint
Tools/Software/Platform
QuarkXPress/
Mac OS
Font
FF Scala

0070
Art Director
Kirsten Dietz
Designer
Kirsten Dietz
Client
Verlag Hermann
Schmidt Maint
Tools/Software/Platform
QuarkXPress/
Mac OS
Font
FF Scala

0199
Art Directors
Kirsten Dietz, Jochen
Radeker
Designers
Kirsten Dietz, Tanja
Gunther, Felix
Widmaier
Client
Papierfabrik
Scheufelen GmbH &
Co. Kh
Tools/Software/Platform
QuarkXPress
Font
Univers

0203
Art Director
Kirsten Dietz
Designer
Tanja Gunther
Client
U.S.U.Ah
Tools/Software/Platform
QuarkXPress

0204
Art Directors
Kirsten Dietz, Jochen
Radeker
Designers
Kirsten Dietz, Tanja
Gunther, Felix
Widmaier
Client
Papierfabrik
Scheufelen GmbH &
Co. Kh
Tools/Software/Platform
QuarkXPress
Font
Univers

0217
Art Director
Kirsten Dietz
Designer
Tanja Gunther
Client
U.S.U.Ah
Tools/Software/Platform
QuarkXPress

0235
Art Director
Kirsten Dietz
Designer
Tanja Gunther
Client
U.S.U.Ah
Tools/Software/Platform
QuarkXPress

0261

Memphis
Tools/Software/Platform
Adobe Illustrator, Adobe Photoshop, Adobe InDesign
Fonts
Bell Gothic, Mrs. Eaves

0835
Art Director
Lucas Charles
Designer
Lucas Charles
Client
The University of Memphis
Tools/Software/Platform
Adobe Illustrator, Adobe Photoshop, Adobe InDesign
Font
Council

0849
Art Director
Lucas Charles
Designer
Lucas Charles
Client
The University of Memphis
Tools/Software/Platform
Adobe Illustrator, Adobe InDesign
Font
Requiem

The Design Dell
0214
Art Director
Dan Donovan
Designer
Dan Donovan
Client
The Design Dell
Tools/Software/Platform
QuarkXPress
Paper/Materials
Cyclus Offset

0324
Art Director
Dan Donovan
Designer
Dan Donovan
Client
The Design Dell
Tools/Software/Platform
QuarkXPress
Paper/Materials
Cyclus Offset

0360
Art Director
Dan Donovan
Designer
Dan Donovan
Client
The Design Dell
Tools/Software/Platform
QuarkXPress
Paper/Materials
Cyclus Offset

The Family Design International
0278
Art Director
Andrew Robinson
Designers
Andrew Robinson, Christine Fent
Client
Well Magazine

Tools/Software/Platform
Adobe Illustrator, QuarkXPress, Adobe Photoshop
Font
Helvetica

0345
Art Director
Andrew Robinson
Designers
Andrew King
Client
Reclub
Tools/Software/Platform
Adobe Illustrator, QuarkXPress, Adobe Photoshop
Font
Helvetica, Snell

0384
Art Director
Andrew Robinson
Designers
Andrew Robinson
Client
The Family Design International
Tools/Software/Platform
Adobe Illustrator
Font
News Gothic, hand drawn

0397
Art Director
Andrew Robinson
Designers
Andrew King, Douglas Main
Client
OTV
Tools/Software/Platform
Adobe Illustrator
Font
Hand drawn

0439
Art Director
Andrew Robinson
Designers
Andrew King, Douglas Main
Client
IST
Tools/Software/Platform
Adobe Illustrator
Font
Hand drawn

0451
Art Director
Andrew Robinson
Designer
Tania Carvallro
Client
YCTV
Tools/Software/Platform
Freehand, Adobe Photoshop
Font
Helvetica, News Gothic

0452
Art Director
Andrew Robinson
Designer
Tania Carvallro
Client
YCTV
Tools/Software/Platform
Freehand, Adobe Photoshop
Font
Helvetica, News Gothic

0687

Designers
Marco Silva, Marta Horta, Tania Earvalho
Tools/Software/Platform
Adobe Photoshop, QuarkXPress
Fonts
Clarendon, Univers

0690
Designers
Marco Silva, Marta Horta, Tania Earvalho
Tools/Software/Platform
Adobe Photoshop, QuarkXPress, Adobe Photoshop
Fonts
Clarendon, Univers

0692
Designers
Marco Silva, Marta Horta, Tania Earvalho
Tools/Software/Platform
Adobe Photoshop, QuarkXPress
Fonts
Clarendon, Univers

0694
Art Director
Andrew Robinson
Designers
Andrew Robinson, Christine Fent, Patrice Gruelrot
Client
First Impression
Tools/Software/Platform
Adobe Illustrator, Adobe Photoshop
Font
Hand drawn

0707
Art Director
Andrew Robinson
Designer
Andrew Robinson
Client
Inveresk
Tools/Software/Platform
Adobe Illustrator
Font
Helvetica Neue

0972
Art Director
Andrew Robinson
Designer
Andrew Robinson
Client
Signature
Tools/Software/Platform
Director
Font
Mechanika

The Kitchen
0915
Art Director
Phil Sims
Designer
Samuel Muir
Client
React Music/ Nag Nag
Tools/Software/Platform
Adobe Illustrator, Adobe Photoshop

0976
Art Director
Phil Sims
Designer
Samuel Muir
Client
React Music/ Nag Nag
Tools/Software/Platform
QuarkXPress, Adobe

Adobe Illustrator, Adobe Photoshop

0980
Art Director
Phil Sims
Designer
Samuel Muir
Client
React Music/ Nag Nag
Tools/Software/Platform
Adobe Illustrator, Adobe Photoshop
Fonts
Chicago, Umbra, Century Gothic, Davida, Vineta

The Moral Animals/ Form Fünf
0536
Art Directors
Daniel Bastian, Ulysses Voelker
Client
Verein Fur Auzptierende Jubendarbelt
Tools/Software/Platform
QuarkXPress, Adobe Photoshop
Font
Helvetica

0537
Art Directors
Daniel Bastian, Ulysses Voelker
Client
Verein Fur Auzptierende Jubendarbelt
Tools/Software/Platform
QuarkXPress, Adobe Photoshop
Font
Helvetica

0538
Art Directors
Daniel Bastian, Ulysses Voelker
Client
Verein Fur Auzptierende Jubendarbelt
Tools/Software/Platform
QuarkXPress, Adobe Photoshop
Font
Helvetica

0539
Art Directors
Daniel Bastian, Ulysses Voelker
Client
Verein Fur Auzptierende Jubendarbelt
Tools/Software/Platform
QuarkXPress, Adobe Photoshop
Font
Helvetica

0663
Art Directors
Daniel Bastian, Ulysses Voelker
Client
Verein Fur Auzptierende Jubendarbelt
Tools/Software/Platform
QuarkXPress, Adobe

Photoshop
Font
Helvetica

The Works Design Communication
0668
Art Director
Scott McFarland
Designer
Mike Rehder
Client
Greater Toronto Airport Authority
Tools/Software/Platform
Adobe Illustrator, Adobe Photoshop, QuarkXPress
Paper/Materials
Mead Westraco 100 lb Signature

Thompson
0308
Art Director
Ian Thompson
Designer
Ian Thompson
Client
Self Promotion
Tools/Software/Platform
QuarkXPress
Paper/Materials
National Velvet, Crusade Offset

0346
Art Director
Ian Thompson
Designer
Ian Thompson
Client
Self Promotion
Tools/Software/Platform
QuarkXPress
Paper/Materials
National Velvet, Crusade Offset

Thonik
0268
Art Directors
Nikki Gonnissen, Thomas Widdershoven
Designer
Rieme Gleijm
Client
Droog Design
Tools/Software/Platform
Adobe InDesign
Font
Avant Garde

0728
Art Directors
Nikki Gonnissen, Thomas Widdershoven
Designers
Thomas Widdershoven, Ben Salese
Client
Raa voor Cultur (Dutch Council of Culture)
Tools/Software/Platform
Adobe InDesign
Font
Documenta, Times, Verdana

Transmute

0660
Art Director
Andy McClean
Designer
Chris McClean
Client
4PM
Tools/Software/Platform
Adobe Photoshop, Adobe Illustrator
Font
Helvetica, hand drawn

Twelve:Ten
0608
Art Director
Alun Edwards
Designers
Alun Edwards, Si Billam
Client
Twelve:Ten
Tools/Software/Platform
Freehand, QuarkXPress

0609
Art Director
Alun Edwards
Designers
Alun Edwards, Si Billam
Client
Twelve:Ten
Tools/Software/Platform
Freehand, QuarkXPress

0705
Art Director
Alun Edwards
Designers
Alun Edwards, Si Billam
Client
Twelve:Ten
Tools/Software/Platform
Freehand, QuarkXPress

0709
Art Director
Alun Edwards
Designers
Alun Edwards, Si Billam
Client
Twelve:Ten
Tools/Software/Platform
Freehand, QuarkXPress

0746
Art Director
Alun Edwards
Designers
Alun Edwards, Si Billam
Client
Twelve:Ten
Tools/Software/Platform
Freehand, QuarkXPress

Underware
0498
Art Director
Underware
Designer
Underware
Client
Underware
Tools/Software/Platform
Adobe InDesign
Fonts
Dolly, Taxi, Sauna, Nobel

0649
Art Director
Underware
Designer
Underware
Client
Underware
Tools/Software/Platform
Adobe InDesign
Fonts
Dolly, Taxi, Sauna, Nobel

0685
Art Director
Underware
Designer
Underware
Client
Underware
Tools/Software/Platform
Adobe InDesign
Fonts
Dolly, Taxi, Sauna, Nobel

unit9
0888
Art Director
Steve Price
Designers
Rory Campbell, Andrew Mackay (State of Emergence)
Client
The Sunday Times
Tools/Software/Platform
Adobe Illustrator, Adobe, Photoshop, Flash
Paper/Materials
Magic Tape, photocopier, scalpel

0919
Art Director
Steve Price
Designers
Rory Campbell, Andrew Mackay (State of Emergence)
Client
The Sunday Times
Tools/Software/Platform
Adobe Illustrator, Adobe, Photoshop, Flash
Paper/Materials
Magic Tape, photocopier, scalpel

0924
Art Director
Steve Price
Designers
Rory Campbell, Andrew Mackay (State of Emergence)
Client
The Sunday Times
Tools/Software/Platform
Adobe Illustrator, Adobe, Photoshop, Flash
Paper/Materials
Magic Tape, photocopier, scalpel

Unreal
0046
Art Director
Brian Eagle
Designers
Brian Eagle, David Bray
Client
Bobby Jones
Tools/Software/Platform

Freehand
Fonts
Knockout HTF,
hand drawn

0047
Art Director
Brian Eagle
Designers
Brian Eagle, David
Bray
Client
Bobby Jones
Tools/Software/Platform
Freehand
Fonts
Knockout HTF,
hand drawn

0049
Art Director
Brian Eagle
Designers
Brian Eagle, David
Bray
Client
Bobby Jones
Tools/Software/Platform
Freehand
Fonts
Knockout HTF,
hand drawn

0130
Art Directors
Brian Eagle, Tim
Lewis
Designers
Brian Eagle, Tim
Lewis
Client
Bass Beers
Tools/Software/Platform
Freehand
Fonts
Clarendon, Trade
Gothic, mixed

0183
Art Directors
Brian Eagle, Tim
Lewis
Designers
Brian Eagle, Tim
Lewis
Client
Bass Beers
Tools/Software/Platform
Freehand
Fonts
Clarendon, Trade
Gothic

0184
Art Directors
Brian Eagle, Tim
Lewis
Designers
Brian Eagle, Tim
Lewis
Client
Bass Beers
Tools/Software/Platform
Freehand
Fonts
Clarendon, Trade
Gothic

0411
Art Directors
Brian Eagle
Designers
Brian Eagle
Client
Unreal
Tools/Software/Platform
Freehand
Fonts
Helvetica

0475
Art Directors
Brian Eagle
Designers
Brian Eagle
Client
Unreal
Tools/Software/Platform
Freehand
Fonts
HTF Leviathon

0484
Art Directors
Brian Eagle
Designers
Brian Eagle
Client
BASE
Tools/Software/Platform
Freehand
Fonts
Univers Condensed

0490
Art Directors
Brian Eagle
Designers
Brian Eagle
Client
The Oven
Tools/Software/Platform
Freehand
Font
OCRX

Untitled

0042
Designers
David Hawkins,
Glenn Howard
Client
RSA Art for
Architecture
Tools/Software/Platform
QuarkXPress, Adobe
Photoshop
Font
Din

0099
Designers
David Hawkins,
Glenn Howard
Client
Pickard School of
Garden Design
Tools/Software/Platform
QuarkXPress/Mac
Font
Big Caslon

0191
Art Director
Zoe Scutts
Designer
Zoe Scutts
Client
Untitled Image
Library
Tools/Software/Platform
QuarkXPress,
Adobe Photoshop,
Freehand, Adobe
Illustrator
Paper/Materials
Board, paper,
plastic outer page

0554
Art Director
Zoe Scutts
Designer
Zoe Scutts
Client
Untitled Image
Library
Tools/Software/Platform
QuarkXPress,
Adobe Photoshop,
Freehand
Paper/Materials
Board, paper,
plastic outer page

0194
Art Director
Zoe Scutts
Designer
Zoe Scutts
Client
Untitled Image
Library
Tools/Software/Platform
QuarkXPress,

Adobe Photoshop,
Freehand
Paper/Materials
Board, paper,
plastic outer page

0196
Art Director
Zoe Scutts
Designer
Zoe Scutts
Client
Untitled Image
Library
Tools/Software/Platform
QuarkXPress,
Adobe Photoshop,
Freehand, Adobe
Illustrator
Paper/Materials
Board, paper,
plastic outer page

0239
Art Director
Zoe Scutts
Designer
Zoe Scutts
Client
Untitled Image
Library
Tools/Software/Platform
QuarkXPress,
Adobe Photoshop,
Freehand, Adobe
Illustrator
Paper/Materials
Board, paper,
plastic outer page

0266
Designers
David Hawkins,
Glenn Howard
Client
Institute of
International Visual
Arts (INIVA)
Tools/Software/Platform
QuarkXPress, Adobe
Photoshop
Font
Helvetica Neue,
Akzidenz Grotesk

0364
Art Director
Zoe Scutts
Designer
Zoe Scutts
Client
Untitled Image
Library
Tools/Software/Platform
QuarkXPress,
Adobe Photoshop,
Freehand, Adobe
Illustrator
Paper/Materials
Board, paper,
plastic outer page

0554
Art Director
Zoe Scutts
Designer
Zoe Scutts
Client
Untitled Image
Library
Tools/Software/Platform
QuarkXPress,

0555
Art Director
Zoe Scutts
Designer
Zoe Scutts
Client
Untitled Image
Library
Tools/Software/Platform
QuarkXPress,
Adobe Photoshop,
Freehand
Paper/Materials
Paper, PVC plastic,
plastic outer page

0556
Art Director
Zoe Scutts
Designer
Zoe Scutts
Client
Untitled Image
Library
Tools/Software/Platform
QuarkXPress,
Adobe Photoshop,
Freehand
Paper/Materials
Paper, PVC plastic,
plastic outer page

0557
Art Director
Zoe Scutts
Designer
Zoe Scutts
Client
Untitled Image
Library
Tools/Software/Platform
QuarkXPress,
Adobe Photoshop,
Freehand
Paper/Materials
Paper, PVC plastic,
plastic outer page

0704
Art Director
Zoe Scutts
Designer
Zoe Scutts
Client
Untitled Image
Library
Tools/Software/Platform
QuarkXPress,
Adobe Photoshop,
Freehand
Paper/Materials
Paper, PVC plastic,
plastic outer page

Usine de
Boutons

0724
Art Director
Chiara Grandesso
Designers
Chiara Grandesso,
Lionello Borean
Client
Replay & Sons
Tools/Software/Platform
Adobe Photoshop,
Adobe Illustrator

vo6

0140
Art Director
Yomar Augusto
Designer
Yomar Augusto
Client
vo6
Tools/Software/Platform
Adobe Photoshop

0209
Art Director
Yomar Augusto
Designer
Yomar Augusto
Client
vo6
Tools/Software/Platform
Adobe Photoshop,
Adobe Photoshop,
Adobe After Effects

0210
Art Director
Yomar Augusto
Designer
Yomar Augusto
Client
vo6
Tools/Software/Platform
Adobe Illustrator,
Adobe Photoshop,
Adobe After Effects

0211
Art Director
Yomar Augusto
Designer
Yomar Augusto
Client
vo6
Tools/Software/Platform
Adobe Illustrator,
Adobe Photoshop,
Adobe After Effects

0212
Art Director
Yomar Augusto
Designer
Yomar Augusto
Client
vo6
Tools/Software/Platform
Adobe Illustrator,
Adobe Photoshop,
Adobe After Effects

0213
Art Director
Yomar Augusto
Designer
Yomar Augusto
Client
vo6
Tools/Software/Platform
Adobe Illustrator,
Adobe Photoshop,
Adobe After Effects

0503
Art Director
Yomar Augusto
Designer
Yomar Augusto
Client
vo6
Paper/Materials
Calligraphy pen,
photography
Font
Hand drawn

0512
Art Director
Yomar Augusto
Designer
Yomar Augusto
Client
vo6
Paper/Materials
Calligraphy pen,
photography
Font
Hand drawn

0504
Art Director

0209
Art Director
Zoe Scutts
Designer
Zoe Scutts
Client
Untitled Image
Library
Tools/Software/Platform
QuarkXPress,
Adobe Photoshop,
Freehand
Paper/Materials
Paper, PVC plastic,
plastic outer page

Yomar Augusto
Designer
Yomar Augusto
Client
vo6
Paper/Materials
Calligraphy pen,
photography
Font
Hand drawn

0505
Art Director
Yomar Augusto
Designer
Yomar Augusto
Client
Superficy
Tools/Software/Platform
Adobe Photoshop

0506
Art Director
Yomar Augusto
Designer
Yomar Augusto
Client
vo6
Paper/Materials
Calligraphy pen,
photography
Font
Hand drawn

0507
Art Director
Yomar Augusto
Designer
Yomar Augusto
Client
vo6
Paper/Materials
Calligraphy pen

0508
Art Director
Yomar Augusto
Designer
Yomar Augusto
Client
vo6
Paper/Materials
Calligraphy pen
Font
Hand drawn

0509
Art Director
Yomar Augusto
Designer
Yomar Augusto
Client
vo6
Paper/Materials
Calligraphy pen
Font
Hand drawn

0510
Art Director
Yomar Augusto
Designer
Yomar Augusto
Client
Superficy
Tools/Software/Platform
Adobe Photoshop

0511
Art Director
Yomar Augusto
Designer
Yomar Augusto
Client
Superficy
Tools/Software/Platform
Adobe Photoshop

0572
Art Director

Yomar Augusto
Designer
Yomar Augusto
Client
vo6
Paper/Materials
Calligraphy pen,
photography
Font
Hand drawn

Yomar Augusto
Designer
Yomar Augusto
Client
Superficy
Tools/Software/Platform
Adobe Photoshop

0573
Art Director
Yomar Augusto
Designer
Yomar Augusto
Client
Superficy
Tools/Software/Platform
Adobe Photoshop

0574
Art Director
Yomar Augusto
Designer
Yomar Augusto
Client
vo6
Tools/Software/Platform
Adobe Illustrator,
Adobe Photoshop,
Adobe After Effects
Font
Akzidenz Grotesk

0575
Art Director
Yomar Augusto
Designer
Yomar Augusto
Client
vo6
Tools/Software/Platform
Adobe Illustrator,
Adobe Photoshop,
Adobe After Effects
Font
Akzidenz Grotesk

0576
Art Director
Yomar Augusto
Designer
Yomar Augusto
Client
vo6
Tools/Software/Platform
Adobe Illustrator,
Adobe Photoshop,
Adobe After Effects
Font
Akzidenz Grotesk

0577
Art Director
Yomar Augusto
Designer
Yomar Augusto
Client
vo6
Tools/Software/Platform
Adobe Illustrator,
Adobe Photoshop,
Adobe After Effects
Font
Akzidenz Grotesk

0578
Art Director
Yomar Augusto
Designer
Yomar Augusto
Client
vo6
Tools/Software/Platform
Adobe Illustrator,
Adobe Photoshop,
Adobe After Effects
Font
Akzidenz Grotesk

0579
Art Director

Client
Barry Masters

0938
Art Director
Paul Burgess
Designer
Paul Burgess
Client
Barry Masters

0961
Art Director
Paul Burgess
Designer
Ben Wood
Client
Bang Creations

0962
Art Director
Paul Burgess
Designer
Ben Wood
Client
Bang Creations

0963
Art Director
Paul Burgess
Designer
Ben Wood
Client
Bang Creations

Wolken Communica

0382
Art Director
Kurt Wolken
Designer
Johann Gomez, Ryan Burlinson
Client
Monolith
Tools/Software/Platform
Adobe Illustrator
Fonts
Customized

0383
Art Director
Kurt Wolken
Designer
Ryan Burlinson
Client
KEXP
Tools/Software/Platform
Adobe Illustrator
Fonts
Din, customized

0777
Art Director
Kurt Wolken
Designer
Johann Gomez
Client
Bellevue Art Museum
Tools/Software/Platform
Adobe Illustrator, Adobe Photoshop

Wonksite

0643
Art Director
Jorge Restrepo
Designers
Jorge Restrepo
Client
Manzanazeta.com
Tools/Software/Platform
Adobe Photoshop, Adobe Illustrator
Fonts
Vasava Epidermis Black

0644

Art Director
Jorge Restrepo
Designers
Jorge Restrepo
Client
Manzanazeta.com
Tools/Software/Platform
Adobe Photoshop, Adobe Illustrator
Fonts
Vasava Epidermis Black

0648
Art Director
Jorge Restrepo
Designers
Jorge Restrepo
Client
Manzanazeta.com
Tools/Software/Platform
Adobe Photoshop, Adobe Illustrator
Fonts
Vasava Epidermis Black

0650
Art Director
Jorge Restrepo
Designers
Jorge Restrepo
Client
Manzanazeta.com
Tools/Software/Platform
Adobe Photoshop, Adobe Illustrator
Fonts
Vasava Epidermis Black

0815
Art Director
Jorge Restrepo
Designers
Jorge Restrepo
Client
Eduardo Recife (www.misprint-edtype.com) Brazil
Tools/Software/Platform
Adobe Photoshop, Adobe Illustrator
Font
Univers

0846
Art Director
Jorge Restrepo
Designers
Jorge Restrepo
Client
ATR Against the Reality Germany
Tools/Software/Platform
Adobe Photoshop
Fonts
Neutron, Univers, Garamond

0848
Art Director
Jorge Restrepo
Designers
Jorge Restrepo
Client
Tartart Magazine
Tools/Software/Platform
Adobe Photoshop
Fonts
CA Aries, E004, Univers

0983
Art Director
Jorge Restrepo
Designers
Jorge Restrepo
Client
Wonksite

Tools/Software/Platform
Adobe Photoshop
Fonts
Univers, Vasava, Caires, Garamond

0984
Art Director
Jorge Restrepo
Designers
Jorge Restrepo
Client
Wonksite
Tools/Software/Platform
Adobe Photoshop
Fonts
Univers, Vasava, Caires, Garamond

0985
Art Director
Jorge Restrepo
Designers
Jorge Restrepo
Client
Wonksite
Tools/Software/Platform
Adobe Photoshop
Fonts
Univers, Vasava, Caires, Garamond

0986
Art Director
Jorge Restrepo
Designers
Jorge Restrepo
Client
Wonksite
Tools/Software/Platform
Adobe Photoshop
Fonts
Univers, Vasava, Caires, Garamond

0987
Art Director
Jorge Restrepo
Designers
Jorge Restrepo
Client
Wonksite
Tools/Software/Platform
Adobe Photoshop
Fonts
Univers, Vasava, Caires, Garamond

0988
Art Director
Jorge Restrepo
Designers
Jorge Restrepo
Client
Wonksite
Tools/Software/Platform
Adobe Photoshop
Fonts
Univers, Vasava, Caires, Garamond

0998
Art Director
Jorge Restrepo
Designers
Jorge Restrepo
Client
Deadline Pictures
Tools/Software/Platform
Adobe Photoshop
Fonts
Univers, Vasava, Caires, Garamond

Yee-Ping Cho Design

0373
Art Director
Yee-Ping Cho

Designer
Yee-Ping Cho
Client
Yee-Ping Cho
Tools/Software/Platform
Adobe Illustrator, Letterpress
Fonts
Din, hand drawn

0615
Art Director
Yee-Ping Cho
Designer
Yee-Ping Cho
Client
Maric Mercier and Jim Wimberg
Tools/Software/Platform
Adobe InDesign
Fonts
Univers, Futura, Apple Chancery

Zip Design

0889
Art Director
Peter Chadwick
Designer
Peter Chadwick
Client
Skint Records
Tools/Software/Platform
QuarkXPress, Adobe Photoshop
Paper/Materials
Die-cut CD wallet

0930
Art Director
Peter Chadwick
Designer
Peter Chadwick
Client
Skint Records
Tools/Software/Platform
QuarkXPress, Adobe Photoshop
Paper/Materials
Die-cut CD wallet

About the author.

WilsonHarvey/Loewy

As part of Loewy Group, the WilsonHarvey team are renowned for their innovative approach to design. Working as multidisciplined designers across a wide variety of sectors, they have won numerous awards and are recognized internationally for their work. Embracing the philosophies of the legendary Raymond Loewy, best known for his work on the Coca-Cola bottle, the Shell logo and Studebaker cars, the revitalized Loewy Group is at the forefront of today's graphic and information design.

As creative director Paul Burgess has 15 years experience working across typography, identity, branding, collateral, Web, dm and advertising for business and consumer clients alike. Ben Wood has been recognized by the design industry with a D+AD Gold. Previous publications by the team include: *The Best of Brochure Design 7* and *1,000 Graphic Elements*.